MODERN MILITARY
UNIFORMS

MODERN MILITARY UNIFORMS

CHRIS McNAB

CHARTWELL
BOOKS, INC.

Published by
CHARTWELL BOOKS, INC.
A Division of **BOOK SALES, INC.**
114 Northfield Avenue
Edison, New Jersey 08837

ISBN: 0-7858-1170-2

Editorial and design by
Amber Books Ltd
Bradley's Close
74–77 White Lion Street
London N1 9PF

Editor: Vanessa Unwin
Design: Hawes Design

Printed in Singapore

PICTURE CREDITS
TRH: 6, 7 (Yves Debay), 8 (US Army), 9 (British Army), 10 (US
Department of Defence), 12, 13 (US Deparment of Defence), 31
(MOD), 32, 33, 71 (US Department of Defence), 72, 73, 83 (BTPH),
84, 85, 114 (Rex Features), 116, 117, 129, 130 (US Air Force), 131
(US Air Force), 146 (US Department of Defence), 148, 149, 163 (US
Department of Defence), 164 (US Army), 165 (US Air Force), 180,
182, 183, 189 (US Department of Defence), 191, 196, 198 (US
Navy), 199, 206, 208, 209, 215, 216, 217.

ARTWORK CREDITS
Malcolm McGregor and Steve Seymour

ntents

Introduction

For every soldier, the uniform, weapons and other pieces of equipment that he or she carries can mean the difference between life and death. Since the end of World War II, countries all around the world have developed better and better ways of equipping their military forces in order to give them an edge over their opponents.

The fighting ability of an individual soldier is an elusive quality which cannot be reduced to any single personality type or piece of equipment. Physical stamina, personal weaponry, mental agility, tactics, air and armour support: within the confusing and stressful 'fog of war', many elements must act together before a combatant can excel.

Yet the uniform in which he or she wears deserves a special mention. The battle dress worn by any soldier does more than declare a military identity or provide basic protection. A combat uniform has to help regulate body heat, reduce visibility, provide rapid and easy access to the various supplies and tools of war, withstand prodigious levels of abuse and, nowadays, give protection against life-threatening projectiles. A large part of a soldier's ability to function as a combatant is constrained by the uniform in which he moves and way his equipment is carried.

Since World War II, military uniforms have developed alongside other areas of military technology, but there has been an increasing standardisation. Despite a vast array of camouflage patterns, at first glance it seems armies tend to use olive-green, khaki or woodland camouflage uniforms which have little to distinguish them except insignia.

▲ *French soldiers disembark rapidly from an armoured personnel carrier. They are typical examples of modern infantrymen equipped for combat in a temperate zone.*

Several factors have led to a general standardisation of worldwide combat dress. In the aftermath of World War II, war surplus material was used by countries that were either occupied or which needed re-arming, including many Middle Eastern and Asian countries, and many opportunistic guerrilla units were unwittingly armed by departing armies leaving a mass of equipment behind. The collapse of colonial regimes was another significant influence on uniforms, as independence movements captured material from their former rulers.

The Cold War

Perhaps the greatest influence on military dress since 1945 was the Cold War, which polarised much of the world into US or Soviet camps. The superpowers' military sponsorship of various countries spread their respective uniforms and webbing across the globe, from the Korean mountains to the African bush, and from the jungles of South America to those of South East Asia. This was reinforced by the major alliances like NATO and the Warsaw Pact, which encouraged the sharing of equipment and dress. The Cold War also gave wide distribution to weapons such as the US M16 and Soviet AK-47. The knock-on effect of these ubiquitous firearms was that the webbing designed to hold their ammunition, such as the US M1967 pattern, achieved a much greater world presence. Now, though its effects are very much alive, the Cold War itself has passed into history. In its place, the UN's increasing role as the world's policeman and the US economic dominance continue to homogenise global uniforms, particularly for those countries wanting the best of modern military technology.

However common broad olive-green and khaki colours have become since 1945, this is not the full picture. Not all countries are wealthy, and after 1945 many – especially Middle Eastern or African states – had to equip their troops with whatever was to hand. Furthermore, standardisation must be balanced with its opposite:

▲ *Wearing the distinctive tigerstripe uniform adopted by many units in Vietnam, this soldier has laid out all his equipment ready for combat. Grenades and spare magazines are visible.*

▶ *This British paratrooper on exercise in the United Kingdom is wearing a laser training aid designed to help simulate combat by detecting the laser beam 'bullets' of the 'enemy' forces.*

specialisation. Alongside the almost science-fiction advances in military technology is a deepening complexity of political and operational duties for many soldiers. More and more soldiers have specialist roles and equally specialist uniforms, and the ever-expanding list of specialisms means that unique forms of dress have to be designed around their requirements. This is particularly true of special forces units, who form the cutting edge of a nation's military prowess, and tend to dictate their own operational requirements for dress and equipment. Thus there is often no standard special forces uniform, only different uniforms for different specialisations, and it is often the best the world can provide. The SAS can be seen in everything from all-black anti-terrorist kit to civilian clothes. At the other end of the spectrum, terrorist and guerrilla forces have a different perspective, dressed in whatever they can obtain from their supporters or capture from their opponents. However, captured uniforms do not give units their own identity, and the PLO in the Lebanon, for example, used leather jackets and the shemagh headscarf to give them some kind of visual unity and recognition.

But between these two extremes there lie a multitude of units with peculiar demands on their operational clothing. Even the everyday uniform is now being invested with features that once belonged only to the specialist. Standardisation and specialisation may seem to march in opposite directions, but since 1945 every soldier has become more of a specialist in an age where the application of technology is as vital as courage.

Few areas of uniform technology have attracted as much investment as camouflage. At the end of the 1990s, there were over 350 patterns of camouflage in use around the world. The Cold War saw Soviet 'jigsaw' and leaf patterns spread throughout many world regions, while the US exerted their own influence through the development of various camouflages such as Tigerstripe. Camouflage is one of those areas of modern military uniforms where standardisation has not held sway. Certain patterns, such as the US M81 Woodland pattern and the British Disruptive Pattern Material (DPM) have been very influential. More and more modern armies have camouflage uniforms as their standard combat dress. Their purpose is not so much to make the individual soldier invisible, but to break up his silhouette through blending with background colours. Some modern camouflage goes beyond simple concealment. All US Army and British DPM camouflage patterns are printed in infrared reflectant dyes which create confusing perspectives when viewed through night-vision scopes. Experiments are being held to discover a camouflage that works in all terrains: temperate, desert, jungle or Arctic, and to develop camouflages which can change colour, like a chameleon.

Webbing

All soldiers need to be kitted out with a good webbing system. The term 'webbing' can either refer to the durable, closely woven material used to make strapping, or the system of straps, belts, pouches and packs which soldiers use to carry their individual equipment. It must fulfil many criteria: the pouches must be easy accessible in emergency or combat situations, it must have high levels of waterproofing, and has to be comfortable to wear with weight distributed evenly around the soldier's body. Modern webbing is more an additional piece of clothing than a strappy addition. The US Army's Integrated Individual Fighting System has broad shoulder, chest and back pieces into which the pouches are built rather than worn. Thus the soldier wears a kind of combat jacket with the weight distributed over the entire torso instead of around the belt and shoulder straps.

Body armour was not issued as standard in a modern army until around the time of the Vietnam War, when it was given to US soldiers to protect them in the jungle. Body armour itself has come a long way since the Vietnam War. The modern US Personal Armour System, Ground Troops (PASGT) features a Kevlar jacket and helmet that can stop even high-velocity rounds In an age when casualties are politically feared by most governments, the use of body armour can only increase.

This book makes a comprehensive journey through the uniforms which have prevailed worldwide since 1945. The text which accompanies each of the illustrations concentrates on the content and nature of the individual uniform worn, but also gives a brief explanation of the historical or military context in which the uniforms would have appeared. Observing the uniforms of our recent history acts as a reminder that wars are won and lost by individuals. Military uniforms are a visual feature of a world that has rarely, if ever, known complete peace, and the uniforms of the future will tell us as much about political geography as they will about military life.

United States & Canada

Since the end of the Second World War, North American soldiers have been the best equipped combatants in the world. State-of-the-art clothing, weaponry and load-carrying webbing give them exceptional levels of control over body temperature, concealment and firepower, and ongoing research promises new levels of performance.

For the combined forces of the United States of America, the first years of the twenty-first century will be dominated by what is known as the Joint Vision 2010. This strategic policy, of unparalleled ambition and scope, aims to take the technological, logistic and tactical supremacy of the US forces to such a level that they achieve what is known as 'Full Spectrum Dominance'. Full Spectrum Dominance is virtually the Holy Grail of military planning, a state in which US forces have almost total and unassailable command of any military situation through the use of the ultimate available in communications, firepower, reconnaissance systems and personnel.

The fact that this vision is even contemplated tells us much about the foundations of US military power. The USA's industrial might and its cutting-edge technology took it rapidly to the position of the most formidable military force on Earth, a force which, though its levels of manpower were way below those of some other world armies, such as China and the former Soviet Union, had access to incredible resources of weaponry and logistics which made its combative force quite startling.

Yet since 1945 the US has learned more than most countries that technology's jurisdiction is ultimately subordinate to the personal skills of the men and women who actually walk the battlefield. In the Korean War (1950–53), for example, the 'meatgrinder' effect of massive artillery and airstrikes against the Chinese and North Korean attacks was inestimable, but so too were the individual acts of heroism and courage at actions such as Pork Chop Hill and the landings at Inchon. Later on, in the Vietnam War (1965–73), advanced weaponry actually proved to be of limited value against the elusive Viet Cong guerrillas, so the psychologically exacting task of fighting in the Vietnamese jungles rested on classic soldierly skills and a strong nerve in frequently traumatic conditions. The UN action in the Gulf War (1990–91), despite the undeniable advantages of computerised weaponry, still took human courage to fly through storms of anti-aircraft fire in the air raids over Baghdad. In addition, the regularity with which US troops found themselves in peacekeeping missions in the 1990s indicates that human qualities once again take precedence, especially in those situations where quick-thinking diplomacy was often more important than outright combat skills.

Men at Arms

Though technological strength is certainly no substitute for personal ability, one benefit of US economic might for the common soldier is that in all US conflicts since World War II, US soldiers have generally been the best equipped and dressed on the battlefield. Recognising that bodily comfort is of great importance in any soldier's performance, the US Army has tended to produce climate-ideal clothing systems for whatever theatre its troops are destined for. (This is not to say that this clothing was always distributed properly: soldiers in Vietnam, for instance, often found it hard to get hold of the new canvas and rubber jungle boots, so frequently turned to the local civilian market for suitable footwear.) As a rule, the US led the way in military clothing technology and webbing systems, and many other armies, especially those under NATO or UN umbrellas, found their own uniforms enhanced through either directly buying or imitating US designs.

Perhaps the most significant contribution the US made to worldwide military clothing since 1945 is the layered system of combat dress. During the Korean War, the average US soldier was dressed in the M1943 combat uniform, a uniform which consisted of lightweight waterproof and windproof jacket and trousers, under which the soldier could wear layers of additional clothing appropriate to his environment. The effect was that each soldier could control his own clothing needs rather than it being necessary to issue a different uniform for different theatres. This layered approach proved itself time and time again, and it is still practised today around the world, but with the addition of today's modern thermal and waterproof materials, the US soldier is even more protected against the hostility of natural environments.

Alongside the demands of climate, the acquisition of new weaponry has pushed the structure of uniforms and webbing further along. In 1964, the infamous 5.56mm M16 rifle was introduced to US troops as standard.

The soldiers in Vietnam soon found that their concerns about its small-calibre round were more than allayed after seeing the damage that its high velocity inflicted on those unfortunate enough to be hit. Apart from issues of firepower, however, the use of the M16 in Vietnam, along with the heavy amounts of fragmentation grenades, Claymore mines, and other equipment usually carried, understandably pushed webbing development rapidly on. In 1965, the cotton duck and webbing M1956 system was standard, but during the Vietnam War the M1956 was superseded by the M1967 Modernized Load-Carrying Equipment, which in turn led to the All-Purpose Lightweight Individual Carrying Equipment (ALICE). These later systems were more durable in a jungle environment through a greater use of nylon rather than natural materials, and their broad-strap comfort laid the basis of the 'combat vest' style of webbing system now used by many units of the US Army: the Integrated Individual Fighting System.

These steady developments show that progressions in US uniforms and webbing equipment were partly driven by new technologies, but also by learning from the actual experience of those fighting. At the beginning of the twenty-first century, even the lowliest of US soldiers finds himself in superior uniforms and webbing to those of any potential enemy, with features such as breathable fabrics, anti-infrared camouflage, plastic quick-release buckles on the webbing, and body armour that provides greater and greater levels of protection against physical damage on the battlefield – a trend that seems set to continue.

◀ *On guard duty during the Korean War, this US infantryman wears an M1943 combat uniform, a multiple-layered uniform which enabled a personal response to climate change.*

▲ *Vietnam's unforgiving jungle climate put uniform comfort and durability at a premium, and the US soldiers there would make many personal alterations to ensure these qualities.*

Canada

Though the Canadian Army is not on the same scale as that of the US, it is still a thoroughly modern combat force which has exercised its capabilities in many different roles since 1945. During the Korean War, a battalion of the Princess Patricia's Canadian Light Infantry won a US Presidential Unit Citation at the battle of Kapyong. In the very same year, 1951, Canada joined NATO. Its armed forces set about various European defence duties with professionalism, though the end of the Cold War brought hard economic constraints. By the early 1990s, the Canadian forces were steadily squeezed for resources, yet peacekeeping duties took them to places as diverse as Somalia, Afghanistan, the former Yugoslavia and Rwanda. Canada's armed forces have retained their standards despite the cutbacks, and its specialisms in conflict scenarios such as winter warfare are well respected.

Canada and the US taken together sit at the very top of the military ladder in terms of both technological supremacy and destructive potential. The US in particular has taken its military futurism to spectacular levels; yet as the shooting down of one of its stealth aircraft over Serbia in 1999 demonstrated, technology will never be a complete substitute for the undoubted abilities of individual soldiers.

Marine
US Marine Corps
Inchon 1950

The amphibious invasion at Inchon in South Korea was General Douglas MacArthur's high-risk attempt at opening up a second front in the war against communist North Korea. It paid off handsomely. Landing on 15 September 1950, US Marines advanced from the beaches of Inchon to Seoul in only seven days, the South Korean capital being re-captured on 22 September. The course of the war was dramatically altered.

This Marine Private belongs to the 1st Marine Division which formed half the invasion force at Inchon, the other half being the 7th Marine Division. His uniform and equipment are identical to that of many Marines fighting in World War II. The fatigues are the USMC M1944 herring-bone twill type, a battledress commonly worn by Marines during the Pacific campaign of World War II, and the shirt bears the 'USMC' name and motif over the left breast. In keeping with the World War II profile, this soldier's M1 steel helmet has a 'beach' camouflage cover typical of the camouflage patterns introduced towards the end of the world war. He also wears a standard pair of leather boots with web leggings. The overwhelming impression given here is of a man in a state of combat readiness. Ammunition for his .30 M1 Garand rifle is carried in plentiful supply, both in the belt pouches and the cotton bandoliers slung around the shoulders. Pointing up from behind his left shoulder is his M1 bayonet, positioned for rapid access in a hand-to-hand combat situation.

Date:	*September 1950*
Unit:	*1st Marine Division*
Rank:	*Marine*
Location:	*Inchon*
Conflict:	*Korean War*

Private
24th Infantry Division
38th Parallel 1951

Native industrial might has enabled the US in the twentieth century to equip its forces with prodigious amounts of weaponry. This was especially true of the Korean War, where communist manpower and US firepower fought a battle of opposites, the rates of attrition caused by the latter ultimately triumphing over sheer numbers.

The US insistence on heavy supplies of weapons is indicated on an individual scale by the soldier pictured here. A Private of the 24th Infantry Division, his basic firearm is a .30 Garand M1, for which he carries a good resource of ammunition in the M1923 cartridge belt around his waist and also in the cotton bandoliers hanging from his right shoulder. Explosive power is given by two Mk 2 fragmentation grenades which hang from the chest webbing for easy access. Other kit on this heavily laden infantryman includes a folding entrenching tool hanging at the rear and a binoculars case over his left hip. Standard combat uniform for this year was the olive-green M1943 jacket and trousers, though here a green woollen pullover is worn for additional warmth. The helmet is the usual steel M1, here worn with a green cloth cover.

By this point in the war, the US-led UN forces had secured a position of increasing dominance over the communist forces, and though there was no major UN capture of territory, the communist North Korean and Chinese armies' human and material resources were severely degraded. The war would nonetheless continue while a political solution was sought.

Date:	*1951*
Unit:	*24th Infantry Division*
Rank:	*Private*
Location:	*Around the 38th Parallel*
Conflict:	*Korean War*

Private
US Airborne Forces
38th Parallel 1951

Over this paratrooper's right shoulder is hung the infamous .30 Garand M1 rifle, the first semi-automatic rifle in the world to act as a regulation army firearm. Supplementing this weapon is an equally well-known sidearm, the Colt .45 M1911A1 pistol, here in a leather holster with a thong for tying around the hip to enable the easy withdrawal of the gun in combat conditions.

Most infantrymen in Korea wore the 10-pouch rifleman's ammunition belt as standard, and the US paratoopers were no exception. The belt enabled the carriage of a good supply of ammunition, with fittings for additional combat and survival equipment. Standard belt equipment, as seen here, was a large combat knife, a first aid pouch (the small pouch on this soldier's left hip) and a water bottle in an M1943 canteen cover. This soldier also carries a kidney bag with an M1943 entrenching tool and carrier. By this time, the US paratroopers were wearing the typical olive-drab/green uniform items of the infantry supplemented by specialist paratrooper's equipment.

The helmet being worn here is the standard steel M1, while the jacket is an M41 field jacket worn with waterproof M43 trousers. Different from infantry issue is the paratrooper's footwear: the 'Corcoran' parachute boots. Like most US soldiers in Korea, and in conflicts thereafter, this paratrooper has a field dressing pack attached to his shoulder strap for the instant treatment of a battlefield injury should he be wounded in combat.

Date:	*1951*
Unit:	*US Airborne Forces*
Rank:	*Private*
Location:	*Around the 38th Parallel*
Conflict:	*Korean War*

Captain
5th Special Forces
Group 1965

This Special Forces captain is part of the Civilian Irregular Defense Group (CIDG) Programme which aimed at giving South Vietnamese civilians the means to conduct their own defensive measures against Viet Cong insurgency in South Vietnam. Particular success was had with the Montagnard peoples, and this soldier is engaged in the training and support of the Montagnard in their efforts to establish fighting camps thoughout rural South Vietnam.

The defining item of clothing in this soldier's uniform is his Special Forces green beret on which his rank is indicated by the silver bars on the badge (rank is also denoted by the white bars on the lapel). Further insignia include parachute wings and a crossed guns and missile artillery badge, both indicating the extent of the captain's specialisms. His green jungle fatigues are standard US Army issue for the early part of the Vietnam War, the first issue of tropical dress which can be identified by the slanted shirt pockets with their exposed buttons. His boots, however, are the later issue nylon and leather jungle boots which the Special Forces had easier access to as elite troops.

The captain's webbing is the M1956-pattern Load-Carrying Equipment, here with an ammunition pouch for his .30 M2 Carbine (which differed from the M1 through its full automatic capability) and, over his right hip, a small medical pouch. The soldier also carries a .45 Colt M1911A1 automatic pistol.

Date:	*1965*
Unit:	*5th Special Forces Group*
Rank:	*Captain*
Location:	*South Vietnam*
Conflict:	*Vietnam War*

Marine
US Marine Corps
South Vietnam 1965

In most cases the US Marines in Vietnam wore the same style of uniform as that of the regular army, though the shirts differed by having fly fronts and covered button pockets. Yet the Marines tended to wear older equipment when compared to the rest of US forces, a fact which has in part been accredited to the Marines' desire to visually suggest their status as an experienced and historic regiment.

This charging Marine has one very evident piece of older equipment. The M14 was a re-designed M1 Garand rifle which fired a 7.62mm round and was capable of full automatic fire (though it was very unwieldy when fired in this mode due to the powerful cartridge's recoil). The M14 was replaced by the 5.56mm M16, yet the Marine Corps still used the M14 in large numbers, often with good reason as it was far less prone to jamming than the M16. This soldier is travelling fairly light for a Marine, simply wearing an M1956 webbing system with some additional pouches.

The green pouch on the belt itself is most likely a medical pack, while the khaki hip bags would be used for either the infamous Claymore directional anti-personnel mines or other specialist munitions such as flares or grenades. The helmet is the standard US steel M1, though here it is worn with the 'beach' camouflage cover which was common amongst the Marines during the Pacific campaigns of World War II against the Japanese.

Date:	*1965*
Unit:	*US Marine Corps*
Rank:	*Marine*
Location:	*South Vietnam*
Conflict:	*Vietnam War*

Trooper
US Air Cavalry
South Vietnam 1965

The Vietnam War revolutionised the use of helicopters in combat. Developments in helicopter design and weaponry meant that choppers such as the Bell AH-1G HueyCobra gunship could move outside of pure deployment or evacuation roles to become powerful strike aircraft in their own right.

This door gunner is most likely aboard a Bell UH-1, one of the most widely used helicopters in the entire Vietnam conflict. The 7.62mm M60C machine gun, could be fired either by a door gunner or automatically by the pilot. The basic uniform here is the standard US Army fatigues. However, in late 1969 aircrews received a two-piece specialist flying suit, a uniform made of Nomex material officially titled 'Shirt and Trousers, Flyer's Hot Weather, Fire Resistant Nylon OG 106'. Head protection is provided by the APH-6A Pilot's Protective Helmet. Door gunners attracted considerable amounts of ground fire, and this soldier wears a flak jacket. In late 1968 a new body armour was issued, called affectionately the 'chickenplate dress'. This had aluminium oxide ceramic armour plates fitted to the back and front which gave gunners better protection.

Date:	*1965*
Unit:	*US Air Cavalry*
Rank:	*Trooper*
Location:	*South Vietnam*
Conflict:	*Vietnam War*

19

Trooper
US 1st Air Cavalry
South Vietnam 1966

Customisation was a major feature of any US soldier's equipment and uniform throughout the Vietnam War, with many troops making adaptations using local sources and their own artwork or slogans. However, this private typifies the appearance of many US ground troops in the war.

The basic uniform was lightweight olive-green tropical fatigues, which were first issued with exposed buttons on the shirt pockets, though these were later covered to avoid snagging on webbing straps. The only shirt marking was a badge over the left breast indicating 'US Army', unlike earlier shirts which also displayed the soldier's name over the right pocket. The helmet is covered in a matching material and has a rubber band to hold bottles of insect repellent. Boots are black leather, though from 1965 onwards more soldiers obtained the modern jungle boot which, apart from black leather toe, heel and lace strips, was formed from a green synthetic material less prone to rot.

The soldier here has standard M1956 webbing and carries two fragmentation grenades, ammunition pouch, water canteen and rations pouch. Three 'Claymore Bags' hang over his left shoulder, each designed to carry a Claymore directional anti-personnel mine. Most combat soldiers would have at least one Claymore bag, if only for the fact that when emptied they proved a convenient way of carrying general supplies. The 5.56mm M16 assault rifle was the US standard issue and a formidable weapon.

Date:	*1966*
Unit:	*1st Air Cavalry*
Rank:	*Trooper*
Location:	*South Vietnamese Highlands*
Conflict:	*Vietnam War*

20

Marine
US Marine Corps
Hué 1968

The year 1968 was a landmark for the US Marines fighting in Vietnam. Early in that year the Tet Offensive burst into life, plunging them into major battles against Viet Cong and North Vietnamese forces. Two of the most prodigious firefights were at Khe Sahn and the city of Hué, and this Marine Private 1st Class is part of that latter 24-day battle.

In 1968, US Marines battledress was mainly distinguished from that of the regular US Army through the olive-green shirt which, though the same material as the army shirts, had a fly front and the letters 'USMC' worn over the left breast. In every other way their dress was army issue. Carrying a 7.62mm M60 machine gun and wearing his flak jacket over his shirt, this heavily laden soldier has several up-to-date features, including the new type plastic water bottles and the nylon and leather jungle boots. His equipment says much about the priorities of fighting in Vietnam. Fastened to his backpack is a set of waterproofs, ever useful during the monsoon season, and up on his camouflaged helmet, which has foliage slots in its surface, he has the requisite bottle of insect repellent.

His webbing is the khaki M1956 pattern, and on the belt hangs a combat knife, a medical pouch and three water bottles (plus a miniature Christmas tree, the Tet Offensive being launched by the Viet Cong and NVA just after Christmas 1967).

Date:	*1968*
Unit:	*US Marine Corps*
Rank:	*Marine*
Location:	*Hué*
Conflict:	*Vietnam War*

Sergeant US Special Forces Cambodian border 1968

Without the trademark green beret of the Special Forces, there is technically little to distinguish this soldier from many other regular units fighting in the Vietnam War. However, taking his uniform as a whole, his elite background in the US armed forces is readily identifiable.

The most obvious indication of his Special Forces status is his shoulder patch. Shaped like an arrowhead, this patch consisted of a yellow Fairburn combat dagger placed on a teal-blue background. The three lightning flashes going across the knife indicate combat abilities on land, sea and air, the latter being reinforced by the 'Airborne' patch running over the top of the insignia. Though the Special Forces were kitted out in regular US Army uniforms, they tended to be dressed in the best of camouflage battledress, this soldier's hat being in the distinctive 'Tiger-Stripe' camouflage often being worn when operational. However, apart from the hat, this soldier wears a standard foliage-pattern camouflage combat dress and walks on the essential leather and nylon combat boots that completely outperformed all-leather boots in tropical environments.

The olive-green M1956 webbing is usual for 1968, while the khaki shoulder straps indicate that he is wearing a tropical-pattern rucksack. Carried in his right hand is the 5.56mm M16A1, the standard assault rifle of US forces in Vietnam, with ammunition stored in his web belt pouches, apart from the small khaki pouch which contains first-aid items.

Date:	1968
Unit:	US Special Forces
Rank:	Sergeant
Location:	Cambodian Border
Conflict:	Vietnam War

Warrant Officer Princess Patricia's Light Infantry 1970s

The Princess Patricia's Canadian Light Infantry is one of Canada's most prestigious military units, with a proud military record which has been maintained through many peacekeeping operations conducted under UN or NATO auspices.

Throughout the 1970s and much of the 1980s, the Canadian Army's personal weaponry was based around that issued to the British Army: the 7.62mm L1A1 rifle (as pictured here); a variant of the 9mm Sterling submachine gun; and the 9mm Browning pistol. The L1A1 was later to be replaced by their own variation on the US M16A1, the C7. Standard combat clothing consisted of simple olive-drab fatigues, though the extreme scale of Canadian weather necessitated a sophisticated layered approach to clothing systems. The recent Improved Environmental Clothing System (IECS), for example, allows protection in temperature ranges from +10°C to -57°C (50°F to -71°F). At this time the combat uniform of Canadian soldiers was supplemented by a US pattern steel helmet, though here the soldier is wearing a simple peaked cap. The webbing is Canadian issue with similarities to the US ALICE system, with two ammunition pouches at the front for the rifle magazines.

In Canada, the rank of trained private is shown by one chevron, with corporals and sergeants wearing the usual two and three chevrons respectively. Further ranks' insignia includes a crown (warrant officer), a crown and laurel wreath (master warrant officer) and the coat of arms of Canada (chief warrant officer).

Date:	*1970s*
Unit:	*Princess Patricia's Canadian Light Infantry*
Rank:	*Warrant Officer*
Location:	*Cyprus*
Conflict:	*Turkish Invasion of Cyprus*

23

Corporal
US Marine Corps
St George's 1983

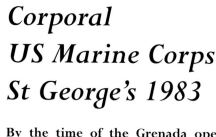

By the time of the Grenada operation, US forces had almost universally adopted the camouflage pattern known as M81 Woodland. This pattern was printed on most items of combat dress and headgear from 1980 onwards and, like the British DPM print, it provided a good general-purpose camouflage for operating in temperate climates.

Despite the up-to-date camouflage print this soldier is wearing, the US Marines on Grenada still had the old steel M1 helmet rather than the new Kevlar PASGT (Personal Armour System, Ground Troops) helmet that was being issued at this time. The helmet here is worn with an M81 cover. Such a time-lag in uniform issue was not uncommon in the Marines in spite of their highly operational nature and, in the earlier Vietnam War, Marine uniforms and equipment were often not as advanced as those of regular army units. The webbing he uses, however, is the thoroughly contemporary All-Purpose Lightweight Individual Carrying Equipment (ALICE) system, worn with a backpack. ALICE webbing was used by the US forces from the late 1970s and provided a flexible carrying system for all operations. This soldier's function is that of machine-gunner, and slung around his neck is the 7.62mm M60 GPMG.

Date:	1983
Unit:	US Marine Corps
Rank:	Corporal
Location:	St George's, Grenada
Conflict:	Grenada Invasion

Sergeant US 75th Infantry (Ranger) Regt 1983

In Operation 'Urgent Fury' in 1983, the 1st and 2nd Battalions of the US Rangers demonstrated their military prowess in a series of dramatic airborne assaults on the island of Grenada. As part of a US mission to bring political security to the island and protect US citizens, the Rangers took the Point Salines airfield after a dangerous parachute drop from only 152m (500ft).

This Ranger is a sergeant, his rank indicated by three metal chevrons on the collar points. He is dressed in ideal clothing for tropical regions: OD twill jungle fatigues; a simple M1951 cap (with luminous patches on the back for patrol positioning and identification); and the leather and nylon jungle boots of the type worn in the Vietnam War. Standard webbing for this time is the All-Purpose Lightweight Individual Carrying Equipment (ALICE), a capable system first issued from 1975.

The LC-2 equipment belt, however, was essentially no different to the M1967 belt, and here the soldier carries usual ALICE items: two water bottles; a combat/survival knife; and an ammunition pouch. His weapon is the 5.56mm M4 Carbine, a collapsible-stock carbine, the dimensions of which lie between the M16 and the Colt Commando, though he also carries a M59 fragmentation grenade.

Date:	1983
Unit:	US 75th Infantry (Ranger) Regiment
Rank:	Sergeant
Location:	Point Salines Airfield
Conflict:	Grenada Invasion

Corporal US Marine Corps Quantico 1985

The US Marine Corps was formed in 1798, making it one of the oldest Marine units in the world. Since the eighteenth century it has gained an honourable combat history, serving in many of the wars conducted by the US, playing a notable part in both World War II and the war in Vietnam. The Marine Corps' legendary status is reflected in its proud and distinctive ceremonial dress.

The Marine corporal pictured here is wearing what is officially known as the Dress Blue 'B' uniform, which basically consists of a dark-blue jacket and trousers, the latter featuring a red stripe down each leg which is only worn by NCO, WO and officer ranks. This type of uniform only makes an appearance for ceremonies and parades or official guard duty and it gives the soldier an opportunity to display various decorations and badges of service and achievement. On this soldier's lower sleeve is a single red stripe which indicates that he has been in service with the Marines for over four years and in that time he has gathered several citations and awards. The sets of ribbons on his chest indicate two meritorious unit citations. The crossed-guns badge underneath the ribbons shows that this soldier has achieved his rifle expert badge and his further proficiency with firearms is stated in the pistol sharpshooter badge which completes his chest decorations.

His smart appearance for the parade square is completed by the white Service Dress cap, with a highly-polished peak.

Date:	*1985*
Unit:	*US Marine Corps*
Rank:	*Corporal*
Location:	*Quantico, US*
Conflict:	*None*

Trooper
US Special Forces
South America 1990s

This modern Special Forces soldier is visually indistinguishable from the elite operatives of the Vietnam War, both in terms of his dress and his weaponry, for though the modern soldier has access to incredibly advanced combat technology, the Special Forces still need human ability to take precedence over sheer firepower.

All Special Forces soldiers take a highly adaptable approach to their clothing and equipment, wearing and carrying only what will help them in their operations. The secretive nature of their combat roles usually necessitates a complete lack of identifying insignia, as this soldier illustrates. Apart from his standard Woodland-camouflage uniform, the only other clothing he wears is a green bandana tied around his head to prevent sweat from dripping into his eyes. His weapon is the XM177 submachine gun, a gun which began life as a project to produce a shortened M16, the result being the Colt Commando, then the modified XM177. Here fitted with the curved 30-round magazine, this weapon found popularity with US Special Forces for its concealability and the power of the original 5.56mm round.

When not operational, the US Special Forces soldiers are most readily identifiable by their green berets. Standards of training are naturally high, with each soldier being airborne qualified and an expert in one or more areas of speciality, such as communications, demolitions or intelligence.

Date:	1990s
Unit:	US Special Forces
Rank:	Trooper
Location:	South America
Conflict:	Not Known

Private First Class US 82nd Airborne United States 1990s

The 82nd Airborne is one of the world's largest airborne military units. Every soldier in the 82nd, including most of the auxiliary staff, is a trained paratrooper, a fact which makes the 82nd a superb rapid-deployment force across many theatres of combat.

Crowning this soldier is the standard US issue Personnel Armour System, Ground Troops (PASGT) helmet, a protective dome of Kevlar capable of withstanding all manner of assault by either shrapnel or direct small arms fire. The PASGT equipment also includes a body-armour vest, worn under or over the blouse. The helmet is camouflaged in sympathy with the uniform itself which, like most 82nd clothing, bears little in the way of insignia. Combatants usually have subdued rank insignia on the collar and the defining 'AA' (All American) divisional patch on the sleeve. If the 82nd's maroon beret is worn instead of the helmet, it will bear a flash insignia and/or a divisional crest. The webbing is the All-Purpose Lightweight Individual Carrying Equipment (ALICE), introduced as standard army issue in 1975, here with an M16 ammunition pouch fitted to the belt and a smoke grenade attached to the strap. This soldier also carries a radio communications set and a hip bag slung over his shoulders.

The 82nd Airborne Division has a distinguished combat history which stretches back to its formation as an infantry division in August 1917, and its reformation as an airborne division in 1942, ready for its major role in the 1944 Normandy landings.

Date:	*1990s*
Unit:	*82nd Airborne Division*
Rank:	*Private First Class*
Location:	*United States*
Conflict:	*None*

Sergeant
US Special Forces
United States 1990s

The distinguishing mark of the US Special Forces soldier is the prized green beret. This carries the Special Forces crest, a bold insignia which consists of crossed arrows, a dagger and the motto 'De Oppresso Liber' ('Freedom from Oppression').

The Special Forces crest is worn on top of a shield denoting the individual unit, though officers tend to omit the crest and instead wear their rank insignia on top of the unit shield. In many ways the green beret is the only item which distinguishes the Special Forces soldier and when it is not worn, as in this case, the soldiers lack a readily identifiable unit or regimental identity, a fact which protects the soldier in case of capture in the field.

The soldier here is wearing a standard Woodland camouflage uniform with PASGT helmet and combat boots. The firearm is also the standard US issue: the 5.56mm M16A2, here fitted with a muzzle protector. When webbing is worn, the Special Forces soldier will adapt whatever is available to his needs, using the ALICE, Integrated Individual Fighting System (IIFS) or Modular Lightweight Load-Carrying Equipment (MOLLE) which are available to the US forces. By the 1990s, these were the most dominant webbing systems within the US infantry and the IIFS was specially designed to be worn with the PASGT system of US body armour.

Date:	*1990s*
Unit:	*US Special Forces*
Rank:	*Sergeant*
Location:	*United States*
Conflict:	*None*

Marine
US Marine Corps
South Pacific 1990s

The US Marine Corps are a regular military unit whose rigorous selection procedures and extensive and regular combat experience give them an elite status. Their undoubted abilities and rapid deployment capabilities enable them to be utilised in a wide variety of combat and peacekeeping roles.

The image of the lightly equipped Marine pictured here suggests the front-line infantry role in which the Marines have always found themselves, despite their naval affiliation. For both night-time and wooded/jungle environment operations, camouflage cream is an important addition to overall camouflage and this soldier is diligently blacking out his entire face. The camouflage type of his uniform is based on the M81 Woodland pattern, which was introduced in 1980 as the standard pattern for the US forces' general purpose Battle Dress Uniform. Here the main camouflage item is a smock with press-stud fastened front and a drawstring hood and he is without the PASGT 'Fritz' helmet that is worn by most US combat units in the 1990s.

The soldier is wearing a pair of lightweight combat boots, and his weapon is the 5.56mm M16A2, a later version of the infamous M16 with some minor modifications and adapted to a heavier NATO cartridge. Though not visible here, US Marines often carry the USMC 'Ka-bar' knife on their webbing, a versatile utility/combat tool which resembles the classic Bowie knife.

Date:	*1990s*
Unit:	*US Marine Corps*
Rank:	*Marine*
Location:	*South Pacific*
Conflict:	*None*

United Kingdom

The British Army since 1945 has tested its professionalism and combat skills in environments ranging from tropical Malaya to the Falkland Islands (Malvinas). This breadth of experience has led to the development of a superior and practical range of combat dress adopted or copied by many armies around the world.

The Falklands War is in some ways the most significant conflict which the UK has fought since World War II. Though the British Army has been thoroughly tested in both conventional and counter-insurgency wars since 1945 , the Falklands War had several elements which made it a unique test of UK land, sea and air power. It was a purely British conflict, not one conducted under the auspices of an organisation such as NATO or the UN. It also required a large conventional response to an invasion of British territory, rather than a specialist response to internal problems, such as occurred in Malaya between 1948 and 1960. Furthermore, it had a great deal of public backing, a very clear political will and an easily defined objective: the recapture of the islands.

These conditions put the combat ability of the British Forces very much under the international spotlight, and they were not found wanting. Though some hard lessons were learned, especially about the dangers to shipping from modern air-launched anti-ship missiles, the task force despatched to the Falklands demonstrated model effectiveness and courage, recapturing the islands less than 80 days after the initial Argentine invasion. The Falklands War showed that the UK had kept all its historical qualities of efficiency, tactical acumen, firepower and aggression, and further confirmed its reputation as one of the world's most competent armies. Yet it also signalled the end of an era for the UK military. From the 1980s, the forces of economic globalisation became more and more dominant on the world stage, and national inter-reliance expanded, British Army operations were increasingly part of those of NATO and the UN, a situation still true of most western countries.

Combined with increasing internationalism, since World War II the UK forces had to adjust to almost continuous squeezes on budget and structure, and a dramatic drop in manpower levels. Despite these factors, the British Army retained both its integrity and performance in a demanding and wide range of operational theatres.

Leading the Way

The continued authority of the British Army on the world stage has been helped by the breadth of experience it has had since World War II. In 1948, the radically different conflicts in Korea and Malaya began, exercising both the Army's conventional and counter-insurgency capabilities. The experience in Malaya showed Britain's excellence in using special forces in the counter-insurgency and anti-terrorism roles, roles which were carried forward into conflicts in Oman, Northern Ireland and the Gulf War, to name but a few, and which established the UK as a force in the application and training of elite units.

In a sense, the UK's skill in counter-insurgency was born out of necessity. The British Empire stretched across the globe and thus the Army became used to dealing with determined resistance from

◀ *DPM camouflage and the distinctive SA80 rifle make the modern British soldier instantly recognisable. This soldier is also equipped with a riot helmet for urban patrol duties.*

32

independence groups and guerrillas. By 1945, many psychological, social and military counter-insurgency strategies were already known to the British Army.

However, it is the operations of units such as the Paras, SAS, SBS and Royal Marines that have given Britain's elite forces such a world renown. The SAS in particular, tested in such places as Oman, Northern Ireland, the Falklands and, most famously, the Iranian embassy siege in London in 1980, have become the worldwide benchmark for special forces excellence. The fame of the SAS is based almost entirely on the intelligence and combat aggression of its operatives, though undoubtedly it also has leading technological resources to hand. Yet the professionalism and expertise of Britain's elite forces are indicative of that of the wider army and a perceptive handling of combat which made the British Army so successful.

The British Soldier

Like every other army, the British Army has a diversity of uniforms and equipment for the full range of its roles. An SAS soldier on an urban assault naturally looks very different to an M&AW Cadre soldier in the Norwegian mountains. However, a landmark in the appearance of most British soldiers was the introduction of Disruptive Pattern Material (DPM) camouflage in 1969. Until 1960, the main uniforms available to British soldiers were the plain olive-drab 1950-pattern and 1960-pattern combat dress. However, the 1960-pattern uniform was also printed

▲ *The US 5.56mm M19A1 rifle carried here indicates that this soldier most likely belongs to the British Special Forces, who can choose their uniforms and weaponry with great freedom.*

in the green, brown, khaki and black camouflage of DPM and from 1969, this uniform was increasingly issued alongside its olive-drab partner as standard. Gradually the DPM pattern became more dominant, and every soldier would have a DPM outfit from the late 1970s. The uniform became the mainstay of the British Army and remains a visual signature of its soldiers. In the mid-1990s, the DPM uniform was comprehensively updated to become the 'Combat Soldier 1995' outfit. This has a lightweight combat suit with optional thermal and waterproof layers, and a new boot with a moisture vapour permeable (MVP) layer to release sweat and reduce foot dampness. The helmet is the ballistic nylon G.S. Mk 6 which has protective properties equivalent to Kevlar.

Another vital change in British Army equipment was the change from the 1958-pattern webbing, which had served British soldiers from the late 1950s to the early 1980s, to the more modern Personal Load-Carrying Equipment (PLCE). PLCE was a lighter and more ergonomically correct webbing system that emerged as the British Army adopted the 5.56mm SA80 rifle. Webbing designs are commonly driven by changes in weapon systems, and the PLCE provided a good configuration for both marching and combat situations.

Despite all these changes, there was a distinct continuity in appearance between the soldiers of the 1960s and the soldiers of the 1990s. As Britain buys more and more into the increasing reliance on specialist forces whose lack of numerical strength is compensated by their mobility and personal firepower, we may start to see a real shift in the way the British soldier appears and, moreover, in the way he or she fights.

Marine Royal Marines Chosin 1950

Only the beret (seen here worn without the badge) of this Royal Marines Commando identifies him as being a British soldier rather than belonging to a US unit. The rest of his uniform and kit is almost entirely of US origin and was issued to the Commandos in their pre-deployment location in Japan.

The uniform is the US M1943 combat dress which was formed around a windproof and waterproof jacket and trousers made out of heavy-duty cotton sateen material, with several other optional layers that gave the individual the ability to adapt clothing according to the local weather conditions. The M1943 uniform was significant for British troops of the immediate post-war period, not only because some would actually wear the uniform in Korea, but also because it would be used as the model for Britain's own 1950-pattern combat dress.

Accompanying the uniform is a US M1936 web belt on which the soldier carries four ammunition pouches, each holding a magazine for the .30 Garand rifle, and a US Marines medical pack. He also has a clasp knife, useful for a multitude of tasks. The choice of the M1 rifle was partly because of its reliability in the freezing weather conditions regularly encountered in the Korean conflict, and partly because it had the natural automatic reloading advantage over the World War I-design bolt-action Lee Enfield rifles. Though this Marine wears mostly US equipment, his rubber-soled boots and blackened 1937-pattern web anklets are British.

Date:	*1950*
Unit:	*Royal Marines*
Rank:	*Marine*
Location:	*Chosin*
Conflict:	*Korean War*

Private Gloucestershire Regiment, Korea 1951

This soldier of the Gloucestershire Regiment strikes a very different image to that of his camouflaged colleague overleaf. Pictured after the battles at the Imjin River, this soldier is more lightly dressed in the standard issue 1950-pattern uniform.

Based on the US M1943-pattern battledress seen opposite, the basic 1950-pattern uniform consisted of a smock, trousers, hood and cap, beneath which could be worn a series of additional layers. This soldier is not wearing the smock, instead being simply attired in serge shirt and trousers, the former proudly displaying the Gloucestershire name. Beneath that, the circular formation badge is that of the 29th British Independent Infantry Brigade, while at the cuff, the two inverted chevrons are not indicators of rank but of good conduct.

The bulbous-toed boots, here worn with a pair of short puttees, were part of the British Army's 'Cold/Wet Weather' (CWW) uniform which, apart from the boots, supplemented the 1950-pattern uniform with a special parka and sleeping bag. The only deviation from British standard issue clothing is the fur-lined cap, which is the US Army Arctic cap, and interchanging of items between the various constituents of the UN forces in Korea was not uncommon. This soldier is armed with the Sten Mk V submachine gun, a modified yet still primitive version of the famous firearm of World War II, and carries his ammunition, with a water bottle, on British 1944-pattern webbing.

Date:	*1951*
Unit:	*Gloucestershire Regiment*
Rank:	*Private*
Location:	*South Korea*
Conflict:	*Korean War*

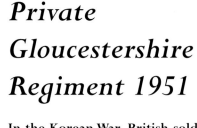

Private Gloucestershire Regiment 1951

In the Korean War, British soldiers' uniforms had to be adapted for conditions in the field. This Gloucestershire Regiment soldier shows a distinct attention to protection against cold and wind, most visibly in his large white winter mittens which were designed to be worn over the standard-issue woollen gloves.

Common to British soldiers in the Korean War was the 1950-pattern Combat Dress, with extra protective elements which formed the 'Cold/Wet Weather' uniform. This soldier wears the additional camouflaged clothing issued to the 29th Brigade, which included the Gloucestershire Regiment, and must have provided a good degree of heat retention when combined with the sheepskin-like texture of the combat smock and trousers. The woollen cap was also a standard feature of many soldiers' uniforms. Worn over the uniform is 1944-pattern webbing, a practical webbing system which carried a rucksack, ammunition pouches, bayonet and water bottle. Ammunition in this case is for the .303 Lee Enfield No. 4 rifle. The Gloucestershire Regiment is chiefly remembered for its brave action on the Imjin River, when four companies of Gloucesters held out against a massed onslaught from the Chinese 63rd Army. Despite their complete isolation and ultimate escape with heavy losses, their resistance drew the force out of the Chinese advance and enabled other UN troops to secure important strategic locations.

Date:	*1951*
Unit:	*Gloucestershire Regiment*
Rank:	*Private*
Location:	*Imjin River*
Conflict:	*Korean War*

Marine Royal Marines Malayan Jungle 1952

The Malayan 'Emergency' of 1948–60 was one of several conflicts sparked by the return of colonial forces after World War II to territories that had been captured by the Japanese during the war. The year 1948 saw the start of guerrilla action by the communist Malayan Races Liberation Army (MRLA) against civilians and British Forces, the fighting happening in Malaya's dense jungles.

The British Army in Malaya most commonly conducted its operations in small units and combined aggressive patrol and ambush initiatives with an effective programme of intelligence-gathering. Heat and humidity demanded an especially comfortable form of uniform and the light and loose clothing worn by this soldier would have allowed the body to breathe and sweat naturally under the jungle canopy. He also wears a jungle veil, though rather than obscuring his face with it, he has tied it around his neck as a sweat rag. The olive-green colour of the shirt and hat and the jungle-green trousers would have given good camouflage in the Malayan foliage.

On his feet he is wearing canvas and rubber jungle boots, a wise choice of footwear which not only allowed air to circulate around the feet but also had the flexibility to aid sensitive and silent walking over branches and leaves when on patrol. The Marine's 1944-pattern web belt simply carries ammunition and a water bottle, the ammunition being for the particularly awkward-looking, yet popular, 9mm Owen submachine gun.

Date:	*1952*
Unit:	*Royal Marines*
Rank:	*Marine*
Location:	*Malayan Jungle*
Conflict:	*Malayan Emergency*

Private British Army Kenya 1953

The Kenyan 'Emergency' of 1952–55 involved British soldiers in anti-guerrilla operations in the densely jungled areas of Mount Kenya and the Aberdare Mountains. The soldier shown here wears a minimal kit, no doubt much more convenient when trying to move through dense undergrowth or up steep, mountainous inclines.

The uniform consists of khaki drill trousers and a khaki shirt, over which this soldier wears a pullover. The hat, ideal for guarding against the equatorial sun, is a simple, wide-brimmed slouch hat. The trousers are closed at the bottom using grey anklets. Apart from his rifle, the only equipment this soldier carries is a 1937-pattern web belt (which probably holds a water bottle around the rear) and a hip pack slung from the shoulder. Standard infantry weapons in the fight against the Mau-Mau guerrillas tended to be the 9mm Sten submachine gun and .303 Lee Enfield rifles. The rifle carried here is a Number 4 with the Mk3 bayonet. Though a fine rifle, its heavy weight made it unpopular for field operations and the shorter Number 5 rifle, which was intended for jungle warfare, was often used. However, this rifle had its own problems, primarily a tendency for its accuracy to slip from one day to the next, a fault which required continual re-zeroing by the operator.

The British forces in Kenya applied intelligent and ultimately successful techniques. By the mid 1950s operations were wound down as Kenya became more stable, leading to independence in 1963.

Date:	*1953*
Unit:	*British Army*
Rank:	*Private*
Location:	*Kenya*
Conflict:	*Kenyan Emergency*

Private
Parachute Regiment
Suez 1956

British paratroopers of the 3rd Battalion, the Parachute Regiment, were amongst the first soldiers to go into action in the Anglo-French invasion of Egypt on 5 November 1956. Though the Suez operation was a military and political disaster, the paratroopers' first objective, Gamil airfield, was taken without mishap.

The heavily equipped paratrooper pictured here has just landed on the Gamil airfield. His membership of the Parachute Regiment is identified through his sand-coloured parachute helmet and the infamous sleeve badge consisting of white parachute and wings on a khaki field. Beneath the badge is a green drop zone flash indicating his belonging to 3 Para. The soldier wears the classic 'Denison' smock of the airborne forces (named after its designer, Captain Denison), a durable and waterproof piece of clothing used from 1941. Webbing is 1944 pattern, which was a three-piece belt and shoulder straps configuration with extensive carrying capability. The equipment here includes a backpack, bedding roll, water bottle, oilskin (for recovering empty weapons) and, on his right hip, a pack of medical dressings and an ammunition pouch. The khaki trousers are closed at the bottom by woollen puttees while the boots are of the rubber-soled 'Commando' variety. The soldier carries the 9mm Sten Mk V submachine gun, which tried to remedy the earlier versions' unreliability.

Date:	*1956*
Unit:	*3rd Bn Parachute Regiment*
Rank:	*Private*
Location:	*Gamil Airfield*
Conflict:	*Suez invasion*

Corporal Royal Marines Suez 1956

At the time of the Suez invasion the dominant pattern of battle uniform in the British forces was the 1950-pattern combat dress. However, instead of the substantial 1950-pattern smock and trousers, the Marine here is wearing a World War II-type lightweight uniform more appropriate to the Egyptian climate.

This Marine keeps with the regimental green beret, though in this case the headgear is supplemented by a pair of gas goggles from World War II, a useful piece of equipment when operating in such a dusty environment as that around Suez. The overall uniform is a standard khaki battle dress consisting of a shirt and trousers with the trousers tapered into a pair of anklets. In the usual British manner, the rank of corporal is indicated by the double chevron on the upper sleeve. Footwear is the tough ammunition boots often worn by the Commandos, which featured an exceptionally thick rubber sole. In keeping with the World War II equipment, this soldier is also wearing 1937-pattern web equipment which generally held a small haversack, two ammunition pouches positioned at the front, an entrenching tool and a water bottle. Held at the ready is the 9mm Sten Mk V submachine gun, a dramatic improvement over the crude earlier Sten models and one which gave a respectable performance. From 1944, it became the standard British Army submachine gun, and features such as a wooden stock, No. 4 rifle foresight and, sometimes, a fitted foregrip, gave it the credibility to still be in use at the time of Suez.

Date:	*1956*
Unit:	*Royal Marines*
Rank:	*Corporal*
Location:	*Port Said*
Conflict:	*Suez Invasion*

Trooper
22 SAS Regiment
Oman 1959

A group of soldiers from 22 SAS were deployed to Oman in November 1958 at the request of the Omani leader Sultan Said bin Taimur. Since July 1957, Oman had been in the grip of an escalating civil war in which rebel forces were attempting to overthrow the government and establish its own religious authorities. It was not to be the last time that the SAS would see action in Oman.

The most notable SAS action against the rebel forces was on the mountainous plateau of the Jebel Akhdar where the rebels had their base. This soldier shows the typical appearance of the SAS in this operation. The assault began in the night, and this soldier's heavy parachutist's Denison smock and woollen hat would provide some measure of insulation against the chilly Omani nights. His fatigue trousers and gaiters are standard British Army issue, as was the 1944-pattern belt. One problem which the SAS experienced in their assault on the rebel base was that their nailed boots were totally unsuitable for the unforgiving metallic rock that constituted the Jebel Akhdar: often the boots would split open on the surface. Firepower is provided in the shape of a 7.62mm L4A4 light machine gun, a reworking of the effective .303 Bren gun so popular in British service during World War II.

Despite battling against a seemingly impregnable natural feature as well as a determined enemy, the SAS soldiers eventually took the rebel base after a firefight of more than 24 hours.

Date:	*1959*
Unit:	*22 SAS*
Rank:	*Trooper*
Location:	*Jebel Akhdar*
Conflict:	*Omani Civil War*

Marine 42 Commando Limbang 1962

The Royal Marines 42 Commando was based in Singapore early in December of 1962 when the call came to deploy to the sultanate of Brunei. Brunei was experiencing an increasingly dangerous uprising from the North Kalimantan National Army (TNKU) and the commandos played a vital role in recovering territories from TNKU forces.

Like the Gurkha soldiers who were the first support troops deployed to Brunei, the Marine commandos would be wearing standard British tropical dress: jungle-green shirt and trousers made from a lightweight cotton. The Marine soldier pictured here, however, has not been able to extend his tropical uniform to his feet, as he is wearing a pair of leather boots with rubber soles rather than the canvas jungle boots that were available to some units. Commonly for jungle environments, this Marine wears his boots with a short pair of woollen puttees, an addition which was advisable when moving through dense undergrowth full of tropical insects. Also standard for the time is the 1958-pattern web equipment and visible here are the soldier's two ammunition pouches and the bayonet for his 7.62mm L1A1 rifle.

Interestingly, this soldier has his rifle fitted with a curved 30-round magazine which was generally much less common than the straight-sided 20-round magazine usually issued. For headgear the soldier keeps the prestigious green beret of the Royal Marines, rather than the regulation helmet.

Date:	*1962*
Unit:	*42 Commando*
Rank:	*Marine*
Location:	*Limbang*
Conflict:	*Brunei Uprising*

Gunner
Royal Artillery
British Guiana 1964

After achieving a state of full internal self-government in 1961, Guiana experienced a difficult period of racial and political violence in which British soldiers were deployed to restore order. British influence would remain until 26 May 1966, when Guiana became fully independent.

British soldiers deployed to Guiana found themselves in a diversity of environments, both urban and jungle. Consequently uniforms and equipment were kept light and adaptable. This Royal Artillery soldier is wearing a rather odd mix of uniform consisting of khaki drill trousers and short puttees and a temperate uniform shirt with its sleeves rolled up. The overall impression is of a soldier who is slipping in and out of roles, and such was generally the situation for the soldiers in Guiana as they moved between combat and peacekeeping operations. The only regimental piece of kit is the dark-blue beret of the Royal Artillery, complete with the RA's badge depicting a cannon and the motto 'Ubique' ('Everywhere').

The web equipment in this case is 1937-pattern, though rather than keeping the standard khaki, this soldier has blackened and polished the straps, belt and pouches. The belt mainly supports ammunition pouches for his 9mm L2A3 Sterling submachine gun, here with fitted bayonet. The folding stock and lightweight reliability made the Sterling a popular weapon with troops such as artillerymen, who may have had to store the gun in vehicles.

Date:	*1964*
Unit:	*Royal Artillery*
Rank:	*Gunner*
Location:	*British Guiana*
Conflict:	*Civil Conflict, Guiana*

Corporal
22 SAS Regiment
North Borneo 1965–66

In both Borneo and Malaya, the SAS proved their capability for fighting in jungle environments. They also showed that they could fight with their heads as well as their hearts, building good relations with local people to sow British popularity and maintain local support.

The usual SAS lack of orthodoxy prevails in the uniform of this corporal of the 22 SAS Regiment, but he is perfectly clothed and equipped for jungle warfare. His tattered forage cap is worn over a sweat rag, providing a combined protection against sun and perspiration. The olive-green trousers and shirt are generic military issue of unidentified origin and these are worn with a pair of lightweight jungle boots and short puttees, the latter being an excellent preventive measure against exposing ankles to insects and stinging plants on the jungle floor. His operational priorities are illustrated by the pouches on his standard 1958-pattern web belt: two ammunition pouches; a 1944-pattern compass holder (seen just off-centre to his left); and a 1944-pattern water bottle carrier (his far left).

To enlarge his carrying capacity, this soldier also has a bamboo carrier on his back, an arrangement which could be adapted to carry many different types of load while being light in itself. The choice of weapon, the 5.56mm M16 rifle, shows the SAS had (and still have) access to the best weapons available, and the M16's light weight and powerful cartridge made it a model jungle weapon.

Date:	*1965–66*
Unit:	*22 SAS Regiment*
Rank:	*Corporal*
Location:	*North Borneo*
Conflict:	*Indonesian 'Confrontation'*

Rifleman
7th Gurkha Rifles
Bornean Jungle 1966

Since the late nineteenth century, the Gurkhas have served the British army as one of the world's most tenacious and loyal fighting units. They are perhaps most easily identified in their khaki dress uniform, which includes the flat-brimmed khaki hat with a lighter puggree and, on the left, the regimental badge which pictures crossed kukris, the famous curved knife of the Gurkha warrior.

This soldier from the 7th Gurkha Rifles would have worn his kukri on the 1944-pattern webbing that was typical of a British Army soldier in the 1960s, generally worn in Borneo with two ammunition pouches, a machete, bayonet frog and a water bottle. The uniform here is in a plain jungle-green type with a recognition motif on the jungle hat to help give the Gurkhas clear identification of one another in the jungle (an identical sign was on the back of the cap). Further testimonies to the tropical geography of Borneo are the anti-mosquito scarf worn here around the soldier's neck and the canvas and rubber jungle boots. As the British forces' L1A1 rifle could be a heavy and unwieldy weapon for smaller men, the Gurkhas typically carried the US 5.56mm M16 assault rifle. Though this weapon had a smaller calibre, it compensated by an extremely high velocity which could often kill by shock alone.

Date:	1960
Unit:	7th Gurkha Rifles
Rank:	Rifleman
Location:	Bornean Jungle
Conflict:	Indonesian 'Confrontation'

Corporal Argyll and Sutherland Highlanders 1967

British rule over the colony of Aden ended in November 1967 after a concerted military opposition by the forces of the Federation of South Arabia and Aden's own National Liberation Front. Though the efforts of British troops to retain the colony ultimately came to nothing (as much for political as military reasons), units such as the Argyll and Sutherland Highlands showed impressive levels of discipline and combat initiative.

Here operating in patrol and search roles, this corporal shows his regimental pride through the visually strong blue glengarry cap with badge, red-and-white band and small red pompom. The rest of his uniform is composed of standard British Army items. The short-sleeved khaki bush jacket and loose-fitting trousers were suitable clothes for Aden's desert climate, and the trousers are smartly gathered in a pair of woollen puttees fitted over the top of a highly polished pair of black boots. Insignia on the jacket is minimal: a black armband displaying the double chevrons of a corporal with brass regimental titles fitted to the epaulettes. Being on urban patrol meant few items of equipment were needed, and here a simple 1958-pattern web belt is worn with two pouches for the 7.62mm ammunition for the L1A1 Self-Loading Rifle (SLR).

The overall impression this soldier gives is one of smartness, something necessary when operating under strong conduct regulations and the eye of the world's media.

Date:	*1967*
Unit:	*Argyll and Sutherland Highlanders*
Rank:	*Corporal*
Location:	*Aden*
Conflict:	*Aden Independence Conflict*

Trooper
22 SAS Regiment
Oman 1973

One of the most distinctive elements of this SAS soldier's uniform is his webbing. Designated the SAS Lightweight Combat Pack, three green nylon packs were attached to nylon mesh shoulder pieces, the breathability of which was ideal for operating in tropical or desert conditions (it was first tested by the SAS in Borneo in 1966). The straps linking the packs were fully adjustable for comfortable positioning around the back and chest.

The rest of the soldier's outfit is informally designed around the individual soldier's comfort. The hat is a standard British Army jungle hat (available in green or khaki) with the brim cut into a peak. The bodywear is a hooded and camouflaged zippered smock under which this soldier wears a woollen jumper for protection against Oman's often bitter night-time cold. The Lightweight Combat Pack had a series of press stud straps at the bottom which could be attached to a belt and here the soldier wears a 1958-pattern belt with an ammunition pouch on each hip. Two other features of this soldier's dress which capture attention are, contrastingly, his shoes and his firearm. Continuing the custom-designed feel to his dress, the footwear is a pair of civilian suede shoes which would have had greater comfort in hot weather marches. The trooper's firearm is the 7.62mm General Purpose Machine Gun.

Date:	1973
Unit:	22 SAS Regiment
Rank:	Trooper
Location:	Oman
Conflict:	Guerrilla War, Oman

Lance Corporal Parachute Regiment Londonderry 1980

The troubled streets of Northern Ireland were a military and psychological testing-ground for many of Britain's regiments, none more so than the Parachute Regiment. Setting aside their undoubted capabilities for formal military confrontations, the paras had to adopt counter-insurgency tactics in both urban and rural Northern Ireland and suffered hard losses.

Snipers were an ever-present threat on patrols in Northern Ireland, so an essential piece of this soldier's kit is the flak jacket. Made from the resilient Kevlar material, such an item of clothing could help stop small arms fire over certain distances, and leave the wearer bruised but alive. Also vital is the small two-way radio attached to the soldier's collar, giving him ease of communications while keeping his hands free for combat. An indicator of the high level of threat on the streets of Belfast or Londonderry is the black plastic badge on the famous red beret – the traditional silver badge could help a sniper take aim – and the lack of a sling on the soldier's L1A1 rifle to help prevent someone running past and snatching the gun out of the soldier's hands.

The basic uniform here is a paratrooper's smock in Disruptive Pattern Material camouflage and lightweight olive-green trousers. The 1958-pattern webbing belt shows the simple priorities for patrol in an urban environment: two ammunition pouches (one on each hip) and a water bottle in its carrier to the back of the left hip.

Date:	1980
Unit:	Parachute Regiment
Rank:	Lance Corporal
Location:	Londonderry
Conflict:	Northern Ireland

Trooper
22 SAS Regiment
Iranian Embassy 1980

This image of the SAS, heavily dressed in a black Counter-Revolutionary Warfare outfit, is perhaps the most immediate vision we have of this elite unit. It is a vision established during the SAS's most high-profile action: the freeing of the hostages from the Iranian Embassy in May 1980, which took place in full view of the television cameras.

All SAS uniforms are custom-designed around the job in hand, but this particular set of operational clothing became almost standard issue for counter-terrorist operations in urban settings. Its advantages are obvious. For a start, a figure shrouded in black from head to foot is naturally a hard target in the smoke-filled confusion of a building assault, particularly as lighting will probably have been knocked out. The S6 respirator enables the operative to be unaffected by smoke and CS gas while the extensive body armour gives some degree of protection against the high-power weapons often in the hands of terrorists.

Bulky equipment is naturally kept to a minimum in a short-duration urban action, so what is needed is generally strapped around the thigh or worn on an easy access belt or combat vest. Here this trooper is wearing a 9mm Browning High Power pistol on his right thigh and three magazine clips for his 9mm Heckler and Koch MP5A3 on his left leg. The MP5 is fitted with a torch which would not only provide illumination but can also act as an aiming guide indoors or in badly-lit conditions.

Date:	*1980*
Unit:	*22 SAS Regiment*
Rank:	*Trooper*
Conflict:	*Iranian Embassy Siege*
Location:	*Iranian Embassy, London*

Trooper
Blues and Royals
Port Stanley 1982

This soldier is one of the three-man crew of a Scorpion tank, a light and versatile armoured vehicle which was deployed in small numbers in the Falklands War. Its advantage for British forces was not only its rapid deployment ability through a relatively high top speed (80km/h (50mph)), but also its amphibious nature due to its flotation screens.

The Blues and Royals were the only regiment to employ armoured vehicles during the South Atlantic conflict. Eight Scorpion or Schimitar light tanks were deployed in total, and they provided invaluable fire support to the infantry in engagements like that at Wireless Ridge.

As this soldier illustrates, their 1968-pattern uniforms were in standard DPM camouflage with plenty of integral carrying space being provided by the four large pockets on the smock and the two 'bellows' pockets on the trousers. Boots would have been the Directly Moulded Sole (DMS) variety, a boot that had an unfortunate tendency of giving its wearer trench foot in the wet conditions of the Falklands. What distinguishes this soldier as a tank crewman, apart from a lack of infantry webbing, is the close-fitting plastic helmet which is fitted with a boom microphone and earpieces for effective communication between the crew. Additional equipment is the pair of Avimo prismatic binoculars slung around his neck and, carried over the right shoulder, a 9mm Sterling submachine gun, which had a folding butt for easy storage in the tank interior.

Date:	*1982*
Unit:	*Blues and Royals*
Rank:	*Trooper*
Location:	*Port Stanley*
Conflict:	*Falklands War*

50

Marine
Royal Marines
East Falkland 1982

The camouflage uniform of this soldier is in the classic No.8 Dress Temperate Disruptive Pattern Material (DPM) and is distinguished by the infamous green beret which displays the cap badge of the Royal Marines. Introduced in 1972, the DPM camouflage consists of black, brown, green and khaki print and is ubiquitous in the British Army.

The official term for this particular outfit is the 'Arctic Windproof Combat Smock and Trousers' and the hood could be with or without a wire stiffening ('RM pattern' and 'SAS pattern' respectively). The scarf, combat gloves and waterproof gaiters that supplement this soldier's outfit were valuable additions in the Falklands, with its frequently wet ground conditions and icy temperatures. Alongside this DPM uniform, other standard British Army features include the 1958-pattern webbing, a webbing system which, on the Falklands, would typically carry a 1958-pattern water-bottle carrier with 1944-pattern water bottle, three ammunition pouches (one with a fitting for an L1A1 bayonet), respirator and poncho roll.

In contrast to the 7.62mm General Purpose Machine Gun usually used by British forces as their light support weapon, this soldier carries the L4A2, a later version of the .303 calibre Bren converted to take the NATO 7.62mm round and SLR magazines.

Date:	*1982*
Unit:	*Royal Marine*
Rank:	*Marine*
Location:	*East Falkland*
Conflict:	*Falklands War*

Trooper 22 SAS Regiment East Falkland 1982

The exceptional package of combat and reconnaissance skills possessed by the SAS were vital to British operations in the Falkland Islands. Their actions included the recapture of South Georgia (accompanied by RM 42 Commando), the lightning destruction of the Argentine airfield at Pebble Island and combat operations at Darwin, Goose Green and Mount Kent.

Arranged around a 1958-pattern webbing belt, the equipment this soldier carries is restricted mainly to ammunition pouches and water bottles, though a kidney pouch at the back makes provision for the carrying of demolitions materials or survival supplies. The water-bottle holder and the M16 ammunition pouches are of US origin and it is typical of the SAS to make up their pack from the most appropriate bits of equipment that the world's forces have to offer. For a weapon this soldier has selected the compact but effective Colt Commando XM177 assault rifle. Even without the camouflage paint here applied to the weapon, it is easily concealed because of its short length (760mm (30in)) which can be made even shorter when its stock is retracted (680mm (27in)). It also has a formidable full automatic capability of up to 1000 rounds per minute. This soldier wears a DPM SAS smock and Royal Marine trousers, and his head is covered by the black full-face balaclava typical of the SAS on covert missions.

Date:	*1982*
Unit:	*22 SAS Regiment*
Rank:	*Trooper*
Location:	*East Falkland*
Conflict:	*Falklands War*

Captain
Royal Artillery
East Falkland 1982

The soldier pictured here is Captain Hugh McManners, the commander of the 148 Commando Forward Observation Battery which served in the Falklands. As a Royal Artillery Captain he would have been part of a five-man Forward Observation (FO) party which targeted Argentine positions for both naval and ground artillery.

The bulk of his combat dress indicates the severe weather conditions prevalent in the South Atlantic. He is fully kitted out in the 'Arctic windproof combat smock and trousers' in the 'RM' pattern (defined by its wire-stiffened hood). Further warmth is provided by woollen gloves and a full-face woollen balaclava. (An alternative to the standard uniform was the Cold Weather (CW) suit, which was made up of a quilted parka and overtrousers with quilted liner garments.) Increased levels of waterproofing were vital to combat the treacherous combination of wet and cold in the Falklands, and Captain McManners has swapped the quite unsuitable standard Directly Moulded Sole (DMS) boots for a pair of waterproof ski-march boots such as those worn by the M&AW Cadre. The waterproofing is extended to the knee by the long pair of civilian gaiters being worn. Though he isn't wearing a Bergen rucksack with his 1958-pattern webbing, it would be carried into the field when establishing a new FO position. He is armed with a 5.56mm Colt Commando and also a 9mm Browning pistol fixed to a lanyard from his chest, both weapons being popular choices for special operation troops.

Date:	1982
Unit:	148 Commando FO Battery
Rank:	Captain
Location:	East Falkland
Conflict:	Falklands War

Marine
42 Commando
Port Stanley 1982

A mixture of satisfaction and battle-weariness, this soldier of 42 Commando is part of the victorious British forces marching into the Falklands' capital, Port Stanley, on 14 June 1982. Though dressed like many soldiers who fought in the campaign, he has replaced his steel helmet with the green beret of the Royal Marines, an appropriate act of regimental pride at the moment the islands were finally reclaimed.

This soldier is protected against the elements in the full windproof suit issued to the men of the RM 3rd Commando Brigade. Printed in full DPM camouflage, the suit is of the 'RM' pattern, which had a wire-stiffened hood and rank slide straps on the chest and back, and here the jacket is worn over a thick RM issue jumper. The windproof suits all had velcro fastenings at cuff and ankle which enabled gloves and boots to be put on and taken off with ease. Footwear in this case is a pair of Mk 2 high-leg combat boots, though the Marines were also to be found in good quality civilian mountaineering and walking boots.

This Marine's equipment is carried in a 1958-pattern webbing system and his L1A1 SLR rifle is supported in the classic braced arms position most comfortable for carrying this heavy rifle long distances. Just visible behind his right hip is a 66mm LAW rocket launcher, a weapon which proved just as effective against Argentine fortified positions as against enemy armour.

Date:	*1982*
Unit:	*42 Commando*
Rank:	*Marine*
Location:	*Port Stanley*
Conflict:	*Falklands War*

Corporal
Army Air Corps
East Falkland 1982

The 3 Commando Brigade Air Squadron was to play an invaluable ground support role during the Falklands War. Flying heavily armed Gazelle helicopters, the Army Air Corps pilots and gunners brought machine gun and rocket fire down on Argentine positions, often flying at low level with tremendous personal risk.

The soldier here is an Army Air Corps corporal who would act as a door gunner on one of the Gazelle helicopters. Strapped in the open helicopter door and exposed to vicious ground fire and weather conditions, he would most likely be armed with a 7.62mm General Purpose Machine Gun (GPMG) and the helicopter would be able to provide a flexible fire base for covering the advancing British troops and suppressing Argentine positions. His uniform is fairly standard for the Falklands campaign. A windproof DPM smock is combined with a pair of lightweight OG nylon khaki trousers and insulated flying boots. The only insignia worn is the gunner's brevet positioned on the right breast. In helicopter operations on the Falklands, as in any theatre, communication between pilot and gunner is vital, and this was sustained by a Mk IV flying helmet which was fitted with integral headphones and a boom mike.

In total, 12 Aérospatiale SA341 Gazelle helicopters were deployed to the Falklands, each one bearing armaments which included two pods of 68mm rockets, two forward-positioned mini-guns and two 7.62mm GPMGs.

Date:	*1982*
Unit:	*3 Commando Brigade Air Squadron*
Rank:	*Corporal*
Location:	*East Falkland*
Conflict:	*Falklands War*

Squadron Leader No.1 Squadron RAF *HMS* Invincible *1982*

In both ground attack and fighter roles, the Harrier GR3 aircraft deployed in the Falklands War distinguished itself as an integral part of the British victory. Their Vertical/Short Take-Off and Landing (VSTOL) capabilities meant that they could operate from many platforms around the islands to provide support for land-based troops and a counter-force to the regular attacks from Argentine aircraft.

The technical and physical demands of flying a modern jet are all too evident in the complex flight suit of this RAF officer. Perhaps the biggest stress on any fighter pilot is the G-force exerted on the body in sharp manoeuvres. Beneath his uniform this pilot wears an anti-gravity suit which works by compressing the body at times of high G to keep the blood supply in the upper body. The only visible indicator of this is the hose emerging just over the pilot's right hip.

In case of the need to ditch the aircraft in the sea, this pilot is wearing a Mk 10 immersion suit and a Mk 22 life preserver. Should an ejection occur, the blue straps around the legs, which are fastened to the seat, prevent lower limb damage, while the Personal Locator Beacon (PLB) fixed in the pouch on the pilot's left breast allows rescue units to accurately locate the downed airman. Oxygen is supplied through the V8 mask and a regulator and all communications are conducted through the in-built helmet microphone and receiver.

Date:	*1982*
Unit:	*No.1 Squadron RAF*
Rank:	*Squadron Leader*
Location:	*HMS* Invincible
Conflict:	*Falklands War*

Sergeant-Major Parachute Regiment Mount Longdon 1982

The Parachute Regiment's contribution to the recapture of the Falkland Islands cannot be underestimated. The paras were at the forefront of some of the most bitter fighting of the campaign, including the violent struggle to take Mount Longdon, during which the paras suffered heavy losses before they were able to secure victory.

With a red beret immediately defining his membership of the Parachute Regiment, this sergeant-major of 3 Para is taking a well-earned break from operations. Hanging from his right shoulder is the 9mm Sterling submachine gun, a popular weapon firing 550 rounds per minute from its 34-round capacity magazine. Here the weapon is shown in its folded stock position, which reduced its length from 710mm (28in) to 480mm (19in). The uniform here is 'Arctic windproof combat smock and trousers', to use its official nomenclature, which essentially consisted of a hooded DPM (Disruptive Pattern Material) jacket, identifiable by the lack of epaulettes and the bellows pockets, and matching trousers. This combat dress was issued to both 2 and 3 Para and also 3 Commando Brigade RM.

Footwear is here the ill-fated Directly Moulded Sole (DMS) boot. As its title implies, sole and upper were formed in one piece which gave it great strength but it had no breathability and so produced many cases of foot rot, and has been replaced in service. The webbing used here is the 1958-pattern, with a 1944-pattern water canteen.

Date:	*1982*
Unit:	*3rd Bn Parachute Regiment*
Rank:	*Sergeant-Major*
Location:	*Mount Longdon*
Conflict:	*Falklands War*

Marine
Special Boat Squadron
San Carlos 1982

While the SAS went on to be the beneficiary (some would say the victim) of intense public interest about its operations and practices, Britain's other elite unit, the Special Boat Squadron, went largely unnoticed. Yet the skills and stamina of an SBS soldier are astounding, and during the Falklands War they were deployed in vital reconnaissance work, even parachuting directly into the ice-laden waters of the South Atlantic.

The SBS soldier here is in full combat gear rather than sub-aqua wetsuit, and generally the SBS wear standard Royal Marines uniforms. It is usually only possible to distinguish the SBS by the combination of parachute wings and a 'Swimmer-Canoeist' badge (the letters 'SC' bordered by laurel leaves) worn on the right shoulder and forearm. This soldier is heavily kitted out in an Arctic smock and trousers, both windproof and rendered in the DPM camouflage pattern. Beyond this, more idiosyncratic features creep in, such as civilian mountaineering boots and waterproof gaiters and a high zip-neck Norwegian Army shirt often used by NATO forces. His Bergen rucksack with attached waterproof clothing indicates a long mission, while as a medical precaution, field dressings are taped to his belt and gun. Wearing an SBS ammunition pouch worn across the chest, this soldier is carrying the 5.56mm M16 assault rifle which is generally used by the SBS in preference to other firearms.

Date:	*1982*
Unit:	*Special Boat Squadron*
Rank:	*Marine*
Location:	*San Carlos*
Conflict:	*Falklands War*

Rifleman
Gurkha Rifles
Western Europe 1980s

There are many items of uniform which distinguish the Gurkhas as a truly unique fighting unit, not least the infamous kukri knife and the broad-brimmed Gurkha hat. Yet being an operational unit serving under British auspices, their modern combat uniform is virtually identical to most other British regiments.

This soldier's uniform is the 1984-pattern DPM combat shirt and trousers with 1958-pattern webbing (1958-pattern webbing has a traditional metal buckle fitting whereas the current Personal Load-Carrying Equipment webbing has plastic quick-release buckles). In his left hand is his poncho roll, while noticeable on his left hip is a handful of natural camouflage materials which could be applied to either helmet or webbing straps. The helmet is the GS Combat Helmet Mk 6, a thoroughly modern piece of defensive headwear which replaced the Mk 4 steel helmet. Made of ballistic nylon, the Mk 6's durability is equal to that of kevlar and it has recesses over the ears which allow the use of a radio headset. It is also designed to be compatible with the British issue respirator when both need to be worn together.

The weapon carried is the 5.56mm L86 Light Support Weapon (LSW), which fires the same round as the virtually identical SA80 but relies on a longer and heavier barrel to provide extra accuracy and range. Both the SA80 and the LSW have come under some criticism since their introduction, and modifications have been made to their original designs.

Date:	1980s
Unit:	Gurkha Rifles
Rank:	Rifleman
Location:	Western Europe
Conflict:	None

Private Intelligence Corps United Kingdom 1980

The Intelligence Corps fulfil a multitude of information-gathering and security roles within the British Army, including the training and deployment of specialist undercover soldiers in support of the security forces. This Intelligence Corps private, however, is an almost textbook illustration of the standard issue British forces uniform in the 1970s and 1980s.

The uniform itself is the 1968-pattern Combat Dress, a pattern which was made of the same sateen cotton gabardine drill or cotton modal fabrics as the 1960 pattern, though with a lighter quality, more economical production and the important addition of the Disrupted Pattern Material (DPM) camouflage print which stayed with the British Army ever since. Soldiers serving in Northern Ireland were amongst the first British troops to be issued with this new pattern. Distinguishing features of the 1968 pattern were a pen pocket on the left sleeve, no elbow patches and a simple shirt collar instead of the more robust stitched 'Storm' collar of the previous pattern.

Instead of a helmet this soldier wears a regimental beret with the Intelligence Corps badge and his footwear is the Directly Moulded Sole (DMS) boot worn by all British soldiers at this time. His webbing is the 1958 pattern, and this soldier uses it mainly to carry ammunition for his powerful 7.62mm L1A1 Self-Loading Rifle (SLR), a weapon which was to be replaced by the 5.56mm L85A1 (also know as the SA80) from 1985.

Date:	*1980*
Unit:	*Intelligence Corps*
Rank:	*Private*
Location:	*United Kingdom*
Conflict:	*None*

Corporal
Royal Engineers
United Kingdom 1985

This combat engineer of the Royal Engineers carries the Individual Weapon Sight (IWS) sniper sight fitted to his L1A1 rifle. The corps specialises in delivering the full range of engineering expertise in front-line situations under enemy fire, and as soldiers they possess an invaluable technical versatility for use in a multitude of combat environments.

Topping the soldier's uniform is the characteristic dark blue beret of the Corps of Royal Engineers, a beret which displays the Engineers' laurel leaves and royal crest badge. True to the British Army standard dress of the mid-1980s, this soldier is wearing the 1984-pattern uniform or, as it is officially known, No.8 Dress Temperate Combat Uniform. Worn with this is a pair of Mk 2 High Boots, the footwear which replaced the Directly Moulded Sole (DMS) boot after the DMS's poor performance in the Falklands campaign. The Mk 2 boot is constructed from a lighter leather than the DMS and features a padded tongue and a better constructed heel on the rubber sole. Webbing is the 1958 pattern which was in long-standing use with the British forces until it was superseded by the 1990 pattern or Personal Load-Carrying Equipment.

The Royal Engineers perform many offensive and defensive roles that are vital for the mobility and protection of the British Army, such as clearing minefields and building bridges or slowing the pace of the enemy advance by laying minefields and the use of tactical demolitions.

Date:	*1985*
Unit:	*Corps of Royal Engineers*
Rank:	*Corporal*
Location:	*United Kingdom*
Conflict:	*None*

Trooper
22 SAS Regiment
Kuwait 1991

Actual combat between Allied and Iraqi ground troops during the Gulf War was extremely limited, but the SAS experienced some hard fighting in Iraqi-occupied territories. Their main role in the conflict was reconnaissance in aid of the coalition forces' bombing raids, but some of their ill-fated missions brought them into direct contact with Iraqi soldiers.

Though operating in desert conditions, this SAS trooper is kitted out in fairly robust clothing, all rendered in a desert camouflage pattern. His head is protected from both sun and cold by the ever-versatile camouflage netting and a major layer of heat retention is provided by the thick, ribbed jumper, here supplemented by a scarf and gloves (fingerless to allow easy operation of his firearm). The clothing indicates the way that Middle Eastern temperatures can plummet at night; indeed the SAS actually suffered some fatalities from hypothermia due to almost Arctic conditions suddenly descending upon their units in the field. Completing the uniform is a pair of combat trousers and lightweight desert boots, while the webbing is the British 1958 pattern. This soldier is without the huge Bergen rucksacks carried by the SAS on their missions and the only equipment in evidence is ammunition pouches for his L1A1 rifle. The choice of the L1A1 is sensible, as the open spaces suit the long-range capabilities of the L1A1 (around 600m (1970ft)) when compared to the SA80's more European-theatre ranges (around 300m (985ft)).

Date:	*1991*
Unit:	*22 SAS Regiment*
Rank:	*Trooper*
Location:	*Kuwait*
Conflict:	*Gulf War*

Private
Parachute Regiment
Western Europe 1990s

The Parachute Regiment's particularly arduous form of training produces individuals capable of carrying heavy loads of personal equipment over long distances in punishing time. This soldier demonstrates the necessity of such physical strength by his carriage of the large Bergen rucksack which could weigh anything up to, even over, 36.3kg (80lb).

The Bergen is a capacious rucksack which is built around a strong, tubular steel framework. When performing an actual parachute jump, the Bergen and webbing are worn at the front with the reserve chute placed on top and the rifle attached either to the front or to the side under the main parachute harness. The actual parachute systems this soldier would use were probably the PX1 Mk 4 main chute with PR7 reserve chute. Apart from the red beret and the Parachute Regiment insignia on his arm, this soldier is dressed in typical British Army Combat Soldier 1995 (CS95) shirt, waterproof overjacket and trousers, all in the familiar DPM camouflage. The high-leg combat boots worn by the paras used to cause bad blistering on long marches, so many soldiers used German or Scandinavian alternatives. However the latest British boot has remedied the faults of its predecessor. His 5.56mm SA80 rifle is fitted with the standard Sight Unit Small Arms Trilux (SUSAT) sight. This sight has a useful x4 magnification and it is issued to almost all combat infantry units, auxiliary troops having to rely on the factory-fitted iron sights.

Date:	*1990s*
Unit:	*Parachute Regiment*
Rank:	*Private*
Location:	*Western Europe*
Conflict:	*None*

Coxswain 539 Assault Squadron Norway 1990s

Numbering little more than 100 men, 539 Assault Squadron is a uniquely specialised unit within the British forces. It offers superior expertise in amphibious warfare, with each Marine being an experienced seaman as well as an excellent combat soldier. This marine is working at the helm of a 5.2m (17ft) Rigid Raider craft and his uniform is characteristic of that worn by the Squadron in a cold environment with dangerously low water temperatures.

Typical Arctic-waters uniform is a one-piece waterproof immersion suit with permanently attached rubberised boots which dramatically improves survivability if the wearer ends up overboard. This suit is worn directly over layers of thermal clothing, and hat and gloves are essential to complete the protection. A further potentially lifesaving item of equipment is an inflatable life-vest, here worn with its standard strobe-light fitting on the left collar.

As coxswains are forced to remain standing and exposed to the elements when operating a Rigid Raider, ski mask and goggles are often worn to prevent salt-water ice crystals from damaging their skin or eyes. If the ASRM soldier is carrying a personal weapon such as a pistol or sub-machine gun in bad weather conditions, the gun receives a 'winterising' treatment beforehand which stops the oil and grease freezing and rendering the weapon useless.

Date:	*1990s*
Unit:	*539 Assault Squadron RM*
Rank:	*Coxswain*
Location:	*Norway*
Conflict:	*None*

Gunner
Royal Artillery
United Kingdom 1990s

By the mid 1990s, the British Army had recognised that its current clothing provision was inadequate, especially when soldiers were deployed to locations which required specialist uniforms. To overcome this problem, the Combat Soldier 1995 (CS95) uniform was developed to give soldiers multi-item clothing which they could adapt according to climate.

This Royal Artillery soldier is wearing his CS95 system to fit cold/wet-weather conditions. The essentials of the CS95 uniform are a T-shirt, lightweight combat shirt, rollneck overshirt, camouflaged fleece jacket, waterproof combat jacket and a waterproof Goretex outer jacket. The fleece, which provides a layer of thermal protection, and the Goretex Moisture Vapour Permeable (MVP) jacket combine to give this soldier excellent protection against the cold and wet while still allowing the evaporation of sweat. Part of the CS95 range is a redesigned boot that takes account of the exhaustive demands placed upon combat footwear. The boot's own MVP liner attacks the primary cause of footrot while the shock-absorbing soles and a speed loop-lacing facility make the boot protective and convenient in one.

Though the boots have a high degree of waterproofing, this artilleryman wears waterproof covers over the boots as a further barrier layer. His weapon is the 5.56mm SA80 fitted with the standard issue SUSAT sight.

Date:	*1990s*
Unit:	*Royal Artillery*
Rank:	*Gunner*
Location:	*United Kingdom*
Conflict:	*None*

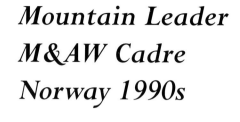

Mountain Leader M&AW Cadre Norway 1990s

The Mountain and Arctic Warfare Cadre of the Royal Marines is one of the most highly trained forces of the British Army. M&AW soldiers all come from RM Commando units and are given a superb range of combat and survival skills for mountainous or sub-zero environments.

This soldier shows the high standards of weatherproof clothing employed by the M&AW Cadre. The white camouflaged snow suit is worn over a windproof smock and trousers and thermal underclothes, or over the standard DPM combat uniform. This layering of clothes gives excellent protection against the adversely cold temperatures of places such as Norway, a standard destination for M&AW Cadre training. Attention to snow camouflage is extended to all parts of M&AW dress, as dark shapes are obviously highly visible when seen against a flawless white background. When the hood is up, the camouflage cover provided by the snow suit is superb and if the soldier is wearing the ski-mountaineering version of the Bergen rucksack, that too is camouflaged by a white elasticated cover. All other equipment that is not white is painted or covered with white tape to match the rest of the soldier's outfit. For example most of this marine's M16 assault rifle has been whitened. His artic mittens are specially designed to enable the user to handle his weapon without risking his hands by exposing them to the freezing conditions.

Date:	*1990s*
Unit:	*Mountain & Artic Warfare Cadre*
Rank:	*Mountain leader*
Location:	*Norway*
Conflict:	*None*

Marine
Royal Marines
United Kingdom 1990s

This Royal Marine presents a good side-view of the British Army's current standard firearm, the Enfield L85A1, more commonly called the SA80. Brought into production in 1985 to replace the older, though more powerful L1A1 Self-Loading Rifle, it has been through several periods of mechanical problems to become a well-rounded combat weapon for individual use.

The marine here has his partially camouflaged SA80 equipped with the large Common Weapon Sight. This sight is not to enhance the accuracy over range as the SA80's limited effective range of around 300m (985ft) means that the standard issue SUSAT sight usually gives maximum possible accuracy. The Common Weapon Sight, by contrast, is a Starlight sight which provides image intensification in low light or night-time conditions.

Though an apparently basic style of camouflage, the modern Disruptive Pattern Material (DPM) incorporates anti-reflective dyes to obscure the soldier's outline when being viewed by infrared devices. Rather than wearing the full DPM combat outfit, this soldier has adopted another popular clothing combination consisting of a DPM smock combined with a pair of lightweight, olive-green trousers. Such an outfit is a typical form of dress for fatigues and other duties where full combat gear is unnecessary. The boots are part of the Combat Soldier 95 (CS95) range and combine a high degree of shock absorbency with a breathable lining.

Date:	*1990s*
Unit:	*Royal Marines*
Rank:	*Marine*
Location:	*United Kingdom*
Conflict:	*None*

Trooper
22 SAS Regiment
Western Europe 1990s

Being so commonly employed in tracking and surveillance operations, the SAS has to maintain the highest standards of field communications, requiring the latest equipment. This SAS radio operator has to transfer information successfully and securely back to base, whilst at the same time avoiding detection by enemy listeners.

The Burst Morse Radio is a vital communications tool for special forces soldiers in covert situations. The operator's message is tapped in on a morse keypad, recorded and then transmitted at exceptionally high speeds. The entire transmission lasts no more than a few seconds and resists enemy tracking efforts because of its extremely short broadcast time. Here we see an SAS operator using such a unit fitted with headphones and a boom mike for sending and receiving oral messages. Though there is no standard uniform in the SAS, this soldier uses mainly British Army kit. The smock is a 1984 pattern in DPM camouflage, which the soldier wears with a British Army peaked cap and plain trousers. SAS soldiers tend to wear their webbing as a 'belt kit' which holds essential survival and combat supplies in addition to a Bergen rucksack.

The webbing here is the British 1990 Pattern, or Personal Load-Carrying Equipment (PLCE) which features quick-release plastic buckles. British webbing is far from standard in the SAS, and its soldiers are just a likely to be seen in US webbing or adaptations from other nations' equipment.

Date:	*1990s*
Unit:	*22 SAS Regiment*
Rank:	*Trooper*
Location:	*Western Europe*
Conflict:	*None*

Officer
Explosive Ordnance
Disposal 1990s

Few jobs within the British Forces can be as psychologically exacting as those done by an ammunition technical officer. Their blast protective clothing must not only protect the wearer when on bomb or explosives disposal duties, but must also give mental and physical reassurance during stressful operations.

This Explosive Ordnance Disposal (EOD) officer is dressed in full protective clothing which basically consists of an Aramid fibre suit into which ceramic or steel blast plates are inserted to withstand shrapnel and pressure injuries. The suit fastens only at the side: this is to avoid it being torn open should a bomb be detonated which the operator is directly facing. One of the most vulnerable parts of an EOD officer's body is his neck, and to stop it being broken by the force of an explosion, a bulky neck brace is built right up to the back of the head. The curiously shaped headgear is the Galt EOD Mk 3 helmet fitted with an extensive visor that provides all-over face protection. Many such helmets are fitted with their own integral fan systems to give the wearer a welcome stream of cool air and keep the interference of sweat in their vision to a minimum. Though protective gloves are available, most operators will prefer to work with bare hands as this gives them the dexterity necessary for their frequently delicate tasks. EOD units have been very active – since 1969 they have disarmed over 5500 devices in Northern Ireland alone, and they are still often required to defuse bombs that were dropped on the United Kingdom during World War II.

Date:	*1990s*
Unit:	*Explosive Ordnance Disposal*
Rank:	*Ammunition Technical Officer*
Location:	*United Kingdom*
Conflict:	*None*

Private
5th Airborne Brigade
S. England 1990s

The 5th Airborne Brigade Pathfinder Platoon is one of the British Army's most unique units. It was formed in 1984 and operates as a separate unit within the 5th Brigade's HQ and signals squadron.

The Pathfinder Platoon specialises in military roles which involve rapid airborne deployment by parachute. Their primary duties are choosing and marking drop zones for airborne forces and making reconnaissance drops. All Pathfinder soldiers are capable of demolitions, ambushes and various other combat roles. The soldier here is making a High Altitude Low Opening (HALO) jump, a free fall from around 10,000m (32,810ft) with the parachute only opening at 700m (2296ft). The rapidity and height of the drop reduces the risk of detection. Over a DPM camouflage and windproof jump suit, this soldier is wearing a Mk4 ramair controllable parachute with a PR3 reserve, and an Irvin Hitefinder altimeter. Perhaps the most essential piece of equipment after the parachute itself is his oxygen mask.

Date:	1990s
Unit:	5th Airborne Brigade Pathfinder Platoon
Rank:	Corporal
Location:	Southern England
Conflict:	None

Russia & Former USSR

The Soviet Army was one of the greatest military forces ever to be seen upon the face of the earth. However, the collapse of the Soviet Union has resulted in political and structural volatility for the Russian military. Yet it remains a formidably powerful entity, and many nations are watching it develop with extreme caution.

The contrast between the army of the Soviet Union and that of modern Russia could not be greater. Between 1945 and 1991, the Soviet Union's might, order and firepower were unequalled outside of the combined forces of the NATO alliance. Today's Russian army, navy and air force, however, are a wholly different matter. Financially crippled, factional and uncoordinated, with loosening connections to the state, the Russian forces are now one of the world's most unpredictable armies, and the threat it provides to world peace is still substantial despite the end of the Cold War.

At the end of World War II, the Soviet Army had a prodigious force of about 11.4 million troops, all gathered around seemingly endless stocks of conventional firepower. It was hugely powerful, and would remain so even after troop numbers were dramatically reduced to around three million by 1950. Yet this was the age of nuclear warfare, when the Soviet Union's territories came under the shadow of US atomic bombs. Recognising that tanks and soldiers were irrelevant if nuclear weapons were deployed, the USSR invested heavily in the nuclear arms race and by 1957 they were testing their first missile system capable of delivering a nuclear warhead to the United States.

The Nuclear Threat

From the 1950s to the mid 1960s nuclear force was king, and consequently the Soviet conventional forces suffered from under-investment, particularly under the premiership of Nikita Khrushchev who poured most military finance into strategic rocket weaponry and personnel. After Khruschev's premiership ended in 1964, conventional forces took centre-stage once more, and began a modernisation programme that shifted away from a total reliance upon nuclear power. This programme was significant, not only for the improvements in conventional logistics and weaponry, but also because the USSR started to expand its global military involvements, mainly through supplying military equipment or advisors.

The first major tests of Soviet military capability after World War II were the invasion of Hungary in 1956 and Czechoslovakia in 1968. Both invasions emphasised the deployment of armour, as under Soviet military strategy the armoured divisions were the core of any major strike force. Though both invasions achieved the Soviet goals, the policy of employing tanks in urban areas was unsound. In Hungary in particular, Soviet tank men suffered greatly from molotov cocktail and grenade attacks as they sought to manoeuvre their vehicles around cramped avenues and streets. Hard lessons were learned, but even today the Russian Army can still mistake an advantage of numbers and equipment for a real strategic advantage.

Apart from Czechoslovakia, the Soviet Army saw little significant military action until the end of the 1970s. In December 1979, the country of Afghanistan

◄ *A classic image of the Soviet Army: an infantryman on manoevres during the 1950s wearing the defining Soviet steel helmet and fatigues, and carrying the ubiquitous AK-47 assault rifle.*

awoke to an invasion by its Soviet neighbour, an invasion which led to a ten-year occupation. The Soviet's principle opponents were the mujaheddin guerrillas, a highly-motivated warrior group who fought an effective war of attrition against the occupiers. Though the Soviet Army had some excellent counter-insurgency soldiers, especially the elite spetsnaz, it was ill-prepared for the costly guerrilla warfare it faced in Afghanistan, and by May 1988, when the Soviet forces eventually started to withdraw, 15,000 troops had been killed and over 30,000 wounded.

The Soviet Union Dissolves

From 1989 the Soviet Union started to disintegrate as a political and geographical entity. Reforms under President Gorbachev led to the overthrow of communist governments in many former Soviet Bloc nations, the fall of the Berlin wall and the transformation of the USSR into the Commonwealth of Independent States. Russia became a separate nation once again, one now ruled by democratic law.

The impact of this process on the Soviet forces was a large reduction in its conventional commitment in Eastern Europe and also on the Sino-Soviet border. Combined with a thaw in Russian and US relations, including positive treaties on nuclear weapons control, the world seemed to be becoming safer.

▲ *Russia's notorious winter climate means that excellent winter clothing is essential (though this has not always been provided). This soldier is wearing full winter camouflage over his uniform.*

Yet time was to prove otherwise. Since the reforms of the late 1980s and early 1990s, Russian society has become increasingly impoverished and desperate, with the economy hovering continually over collapse while corruption and crime expand on an almost industrialised scale. The once proud Soviet forces are now in a perilous and agitated state, with many soldiers going hungry, unfed and unpaid while private armies prosper under nationally powerful criminals. The result has been the effective breakdown of the united Soviet Army, and the current armed forces are split between 15–24 different organisations, all with few checks on the extent of their power apart from the mood and funding of the President himself.

This climate has led to several deeply unpopular and bloody wars in former Soviet Republics such as Chechnya, Georgia and Moldova, wars which have pushed military morale to great depths and cost tens of thousands of lives. Ironically, despite all these conditions, some areas of the Russian military, such as missile technology and aircraft manufacture, have continued to receive investment and development, though the lot of the general footsoldier is usually poor. Since the break-up of the Soviet Union, there has been something of an explosion in uniform design, with each new republic issuing their own uniforms, but the old style clothing naturally remains common.

It would be difficult to predict how the Russian Army will develop over the first half of the twenty-first century. Socially, politically and economically Russia is an unstable country and it remains to be seen how the military will fit into such turbulent conditions. What is certain is that as such vast amounts of nuclear and conventional weaponry remain active, the world will watch the Russian future with real vigilance.

Junior Sergeant Soviet Armoured Regiment 1945

As soon as World War II ended, the armoured regiments of the Soviet Union became a pivotal force in the new conditions of the Cold War. Central to Soviet doctrine were the tactics of the heavy armoured offensive that they had developed in the war. Had conflict between East and West arisen, Soviet tank divisions would have tried to punch through NATO's forward defence lines using Blitz-krieg style tactics to make a gap through which to pur the men and firepower of the motor rifle divisions.

As you would expect so early after the war, the Soviet soldiers of the late 1940s had little to distringuish them from the wartime troops. The tankman pictured here wears a hat which actually predates 1939, being a sun hat issued to troops in 1938 in the commands of Central Asia, North Caucasia and Trans Caucasia. The rest of his uniform follows a standard Soviet pattern which would be present in the Soviet Army well into the 1970s, consisting of a thigh length tunic with stand-or-fall collar, wide-leg trousers and the pull-on laceless black boots. This soldier's rank is that of junior sergeant, and his collar displays the red and black arm-of-service colours worn by tank and artillery soldiers. As a tank crew member, he carries very little equipment.

Also visible on the soldier's collar is a small metal tank badge. Metal badges were worn by all the forces of the Soviet Union as an extra means of identification and to develop a sense of regimental pride.

Date:	*1945*
Unit:	*Armoured Regiment*
Rank:	*Junior Sergeant*
Location:	*East Germany*
Conflict:	*None*

Private
Soviet Army
Budapest 1956

The Hungarian uprising of 1956 taught the Soviet military severe lessons about the dangers of sending armoured divisions into urban conflicts. Attempting to crush Hungarian protests against the incumbent communist regime, the Soviets deployed tanks directly onto the streets of Budapest, the result being the loss of some 40 tanks and many men in the confined avenues and squares of the city.

Later in the uprising, the Soviets realised some of their mistakes and sent larger numbers of support infantry into Budapest in armoured personal carriers. Though belonging to this mid 1950s conflict, the soldier pictured here is dressed in a uniform of identical design to that worn by Soviet troops throughout World War II. Standard Soviet field uniform until about 1970 consisted of a high-collar tunic with four buttons and shoulder straps, and matching breeches and high, laceless black leather boots. The uniform is in olive green and features a side cap displaying the communist red star. Over the right shoulder is hanging a gas mask case and on his belt is an ammunition pouch for his 7.62mm AK-47 assault rifle. The initial battering which the Soviet forces took in Hungary was reversed in early November. Deploying a truly massive force of 12 divisions, the Soviet Army resumed the assault, but this time the support of ground troops protected the armoured commitments. In only a few days Hungarian resistance was effectively annulled.

Date:	1956
Unit:	Soviet Infantry
Rank:	Private
Location:	Budapest
Conflict:	Hungarian Uprising

Tank Driver Soviet Armoured Forces 1968

This Soviet soldier of 1968 is instantly recognisable as a tank crewman by his black two-piece uniform (later to become one-piece black overalls) and padded helmet. As part of the three-man crew of a T55 main battle tank, he participated in the Soviet Union's forcible occupation of Czecho-slovakia in the spring of 1968.

The ribbed helmet is not just a protective feature, but contains communication headphones, while the socket hanging down his left shoulder is for a RT/IC radio-to-vehicle transmitter. Around his neck there is also a fitting for a throat microphone, though generally speaking, in Cold War operational manoeuvres radio silence would be kept until an actual attack had started. The black overalls worn as standard by the Soviet tank men also became standard wear for the crews of Armoured Personnel Carriers (APCs), and underneath this soldier's jacket is worn a khaki Soviet Army shirt of regular infantry type. Typically, if the soldier belonged to an armoured regiment he would wear black shoulder boards with the gold lettering 'CA' (Soviet Army) under his rank insignia, while those belonging to Motor Rifle Regiments wore the infantry shoulder boards. The uniform is completed by the classic Soviet black boots, which crewman often wore with felt winding underneath rather than socks. This soldier is armed with the ever-reliable AK-47, though this was developed into the shorter 5.45mm AKSU specifically for use by tank and APC crewmen.

Date:	*1968*
Unit:	*Soviet tank forces*
Rank:	*Driver*
Location:	*Prague*
Conflict:	*Invasion of Czechoslovakia*

Paratrooper
Soviet Airborne Forces
Kabul 1979

Soviet paratroopers were deployed in Afghanistan right from the very start of the war in 1979. The troops of various Guards Airborne Divisions were used in conjunction with spetsnaz special forces to perform the Soviet invasion's opening attack-and-capture operations around Kabul and they went on to lead several major offensives against the mujaheddin guerrillas.

Though not officially classed as special forces soldiers, in practical terms the Soviet paratroopers held this status, not least because of their training in night, mountain or counter-insurgency operations. Thus it is noticeable in the case of the soldier pictured here that he is wearing the blue and white striped tee shirt normally associated with spetsnaz or the Soviet Naval Infantry. In operational circumstances, the Soviet paratroopers would generally be dressed in the standard uniforms of the Soviet infantry, though this soldier is wearing an all-in-one padded jump suit with head protector (over which a helmet would be usually be worn). The jump suit would give good thermal protection against the bitter air temperatures that the paratrooper would experience when jumping over the high Afghan mountains and plains. On the soldier's belt he has a pistol, probably a 9mm APS, while over his right hip he has a simple bag for basic supplies and rations.

The primary airborne divisions deployed by the Soviet Union in Afghanistan were the 6th, 103rd, 104th, and 105th Guards Airborne Divisions.

Date:	*1979*
Unit:	*Soviet Airborne Forces*
Rank:	*Paratrooper*
Location:	*Around Kabul*
Conflict:	*Afghan War*

Sergeant-Major Motorised Rifle Bn W. Afghanistan 1980

After many years of interference in Afghanistan's political life, the Soviet Union invaded on 24 December 1979 in an attempt to maintain a pro-Soviet regime against the Muslim mujaheddin freedom fighters. By 1989 the Soviet forces were withdrawing, having suffered ten years under the highly motivated attacks of the Afghan guerrillas with mounting casualties, cruel weather and a weakening political will back in Moscow.

The uniform of the Soviet infantryman, being born out of the Russian climate, was intended to provide a good measure of protection against the cold. Pictured here is a sergeant-major of a motorised rifle battalion wearing the distinctive grey brown fly-fronted overcoat and the fur hat, or ushanka. The rank is displayed on the shoulder straps, while arm of service is indicated by the collar patches. Just as distinctive as the uniform is the 7.62mm AKM assault rifle, a successor to the AK-47 which started one of the most successful and pervasive series of firearms this century, mainly due its reliability and effective firepower under combat conditions. (The AKM can be distinguished from the AK-47 by the recess situated just above the magazine housing.) The sidearm carried here is the standard issue Makarov PM and hanging on the same belt is an AKM bayonet (with wire-cutting capability), a respirator case for gas mask and filter unit, and, on the soldier's right hip, an AKM ammunition pouch. Soviet soldiers in Afghanistan were also often seen carrying a backpack.

Date:	*1980*
Unit:	*Motorised Rifle Battalion*
Rank:	*Sergeant-Major*
Location:	*West Afghanistan*
Conflict:	*Afghan War*

Sergeant Spetsnaz Afghan Mountains 1986

Spetsnaz Special Forces soldiers were used throughout the conflict in Afghanistan, mainly in ambush or surveillance roles. Their success was mixed, however, with Spetsnaz losing several units to the resourceful and defiant mujaheddin guerrillas.

The Spetsnaz soldier pictured on page 82 is evidently on a training exercise, yet this trooper is in a much more operational mode of dress. All elite units dress to requirements, and this soldier is wearing a set of hooded overalls rendered in a foliage-pattern camouflage typical of Soviet Special Forces. Spetsnaz combatants have to demonstrate complete self-reliance, so they tend to travel light when on combat missions, living off the land and captured supplies. This soldier has a kidney pouch slung over his shoulder to contain his basic supplies while on his webbing belt he has a AK-series bayonet in its specially designed wire-cutting scabbard, an ammunition pouch and, at the front of his waist, a 9mm PRI automatic pistol. The holster of the pistol features a spare magazine holder on its front. As a main weapon he is carrying an AKS-74 with its standard folding stock. One final, and rather anachronistic, feature of this soldier's dress is his footwear, a pair of calf-length high boots. This type of boot had a long history with Soviet Forces and back into the days of Imperial Russia. They were commonly worn throughout the World War II and the fact that this soldier is still wearing them in the 1980s indicates their basic comfort as a combat boot.

Date:	*1986*
Unit:	*Spetsnaz*
Rank:	*Sergeant*
Location:	*Afghan Mountains*
Conflict:	*Afghan War*

Sergeant Ministry of State Security 1988

Capped by the real fur ushanka hat (enlisted men of regular units wore synthetic fur), this soldier presents a formidable vision of authority and military confidence as a representative of the much feared Ministry of State Security (MVD).

When not wearing the ushanka, Soviet troops in the early 1990s would generally wear either the SSh-40 or newer SSh-60 helmet, or a simple forage cap which replaced the pilotka sidecap in 1984. However, MVD troops could also be seen in broad-brimmed officer-style caps which featured a russet band to indicate MVD membership. The thick sheepskin coat that this soldier is wearing were usually only issued to officers, yet the authority that the Ministry of State Security carried would give access to the best of Soviet supplies. Nevertheless, enlisted men in regular units were issued with such coats when operating in regions with particularly severe winter weather. This guard is generally kitted out in the standard winter field dress of the infantry, with high pull-on leather boots, a leather belt with the Soviet star on the buckle, and a holster on his right hip for his pistol, most probably a 9mm Makarov, though pistols were usually only issued to senior officers. On the strap going over his right shoulder no doubt hangs the faithful AKM assault rifle. In Soviet Army regulations, there were four types of uniform: Parade Walking-Out Dress; Everyday Dress; Field Dress; and Work Dress. Each of these types is subdivided into winter and summer variants.

Date:	*1988*
Unit:	*Ministry of State Security*
Rank:	*Sergeant*
Location:	*Moscow*
Conflict:	*None*

Corporal
Soviet Naval Infantry
Northern Russia 1980s

Executing a dramatic karate side-kick, this soldier's physical control and aggression indicate the elite capabilities of the Naval Infantry, the oldest of the former Soviet Union's special forces.

The defining emblem of the Soviet Naval Infantry is the fouled-anchor cap badge worn by all ranks on the traditional black beret, though lower ranks can also be seen with a small red star. A red triangular flash bearing another

anchor motif is often worn on the beret. In combat a black steel helmet is worn with a red star in the centre and an anchor stencilled on the left.

A trademark piece of clothing for the Naval Infantry is a blue and white striped T-shirt worn by most Soviet Special Forces, though here this is covered by a one-piece lightweight camouflage combat uniform. Naval Infantry units which have Guard status also wear a Guards badge over their right uniform pocket and all usually have a gold anchor insignia on the sleeve. Markings on the broad steel belt buckle indicate to which of four naval fleets the soldier belongs (Northern, Baltic, Black Sea and Pacific). Clutched in his hands are bayonets for the AK series of firearms which can also act as wire-cutters.

Date:	*1980s*
Unit:	*Naval Infantry*
Rank:	*Corporal*
Location:	*Northern Russia*
Conflict:	*None*

Sergeant Spetsnaz Russia 1990s

Spetsnaz is a contraction of the words 'Spetsialnoye Nazhacheniye' which are translated as 'special-purpose'. The soldiers who work under the spetsnaz banner are the most highly trained military personnel of the former Soviet Union and modern-day Russia, with operational capabilities that range from infiltration and surveillance to assassination and airborne operations.

As a secretive unit, there is no standard uniform, the spetsnaz soldier instead wearing whatever is suited to his or her operational secrecy. The soldier pictured here has no distinguishing insignia or markings (apart from the usual army belt), though this in itself may well be a good indicator of his spetsnaz status. When abroad, spetsnaz soldiers will often wear the uniforms of a locally based unit, but generally they wear the standard beret of an airborne soldier. This can act as an identifier, however, for airborne soldiers wear a Guards badge on their blue epaulettes, a feature which the spetsnaz do not duplicate. This soldier, engaged in unarmed combat training, shows variety in his webbing and equipment arrangements. On his back is strapped a 5.54mm AKS-74 assault rifle, a high velocity weapon fitted with a recognisable muzzle brake to stop climb during automatic fire. In his right hand is an AK-series bayonet/combat knife.

The generally lightweight approach to uniform and equipment demonstrated by this Spetsnaz soldier is typical of the unit, which places a high premium on total self-reliance.

Date:	*1990s*
Unit:	*Spetsnaz*
Rank:	*Sergeant*
Location:	*Russia*
Conflict:	*None*

Europe

The diversity within Europe means that the standards of military clothing and equipment have varied considerably between countries. Yet several major conflicts and a constant battle against terrorism have generally kept European standards of combat dress and weaponry high, often relying on US or Soviet supplies to stay ahead.

83

Modern Military Uniforms

Until the 1980s, Europe's military situation was split along fairly definite physical borders, the borders of the Cold War. World War II ended in 1945 with almost all of mainland Europe reeling from the traumas of occupation, liberation or devastation. Yet almost immediately the antagonisms between the Soviet Union and the western Allies set in train continental divisions which would make sure military preparedness remained high on the agenda for much of the rest of the century. The Cold War was not the sole cause of military activity upon the European states, for many had colonial outposts to maintain, yet even European colonial troubles often had their context in this more global power struggle.

By 1949, Soviet-led communism had advanced deeply into Eastern Europe so as to form a communist border from the Baltic to the Adriatic. East Germany, Poland, Czechoslovakia, Hungary, Romania, Bulgaria and Albania were all now Soviet satellite states, while Yugoslavia completed the southern perimeter of this territory as an independent communist state. This frontier, holding back the massed ranks of the Soviet army, naturally led the West towards the formation of their own protective association, namely the North Atlantic Treaty Organisation (NATO). NATO was created in 1949 and consisted of 12 nations (the US and Canada being the non-European members) who were committed to principles of mutual defence should one or more member be threatened.

With NATO in place, Europe's eastern and western military forces faced each other with huge combined conventional forces (though the Cold War was much more dominated by the mutual threat of nuclear weapons).

Despite the massive investment in conventional forces, particularly in airpower and armoured vehicles, the Cold War armies never met in face-to-face conflict. Yet this is far from saying that the European nations stayed militarily inactive. The Cold War's dimensions spread right around the globe, and in 1950 six European nations entered the Korean War as part of the UN forces fighting the North Korean and Chinese armies. Though this conflict was on a bigger scale than many that succeeded it, in terms of individual nations much more bloody wars were to come in the post-World War II years, particularly in the context of European colonial territories.

France, for instance, was to fight a costly war in Indochina (1946–54) in which it lost 21,000 soldiers, followed by a bitter counter-insurgency conflict in Algeria (1954–62) which cost another 17,500 French lives. In addition to foreign and civil conflicts, Europe also experienced significant levels of terrorism on its homelands, and consequently became a breeding ground for some of the world's most elite counter-terrorism units. France's GIGN, Germany's GSG-9, the Italian GIS and the Spanish GEO are just some of the units which have captured world respect through

◄ *Wearing full parade uniform and carrying a FAMAS F1 rifle, this soldier of the French Foreign Legion demonstrates the importance of the uniform as proof of a proud military tradition.*

their levels of training and combat professionalism. Investment in such units will doubtless remain high, and co-operation between European police forces and military units ensures that expertise is generally shared.

The break-up of the Soviet Union started to inexorably push military investment away from massed defensive armies towards smaller, more mobile forces with superior tactical firepower. Ironically, as these changes were taking place, many European countries were called upon to fight in the Gulf War of 1990–91, a thoroughly conventional war which relied on massed air attacks and armoured assaults across the flat desert plains of Kuwait and Iraq. That formidable success gave a massive boost to European military confidence, yet the acute desire to avoid casualties meant that ground troop combat involvements were kept to a minimum.

The Former Yugoslavia

This desire was repeated in 1999 when NATO became involved in its first conflict as an organisation: the bombing of Serbia in an attempt to return the forcibly expelled population of Kosovo. The break-up of the former Yugoslavia was one of Europe's most bloody events since World War II. Though the countries involved had not insignificant amounts of heavy weaponry, much of the high death toll was caused by local troop action combined with a vicious persecution of ethnic groups of a type not seen in Europe since the days of Hitler. Some of the appalling acts of mass murder brought the European community into action through the UN or NATO, though prior to the Kosovo action, there was little that the European armies could do to prevent the killing.

The involvements of European armies in the former Yugoslavia illustrates one of their most important past and future roles: peacekeeping. Many European forces have a wide experience of peacekeeping in contested places and regions throughout the Middle East, Africa and southern Europe, mostly under UN jurisdiction. These operations have provided some armies with significant active-service experience, especially armies of neutral countries such as Sweden. Peacekeeping roles at the end of the 1990s seemed to be on the increase as governments trod an increasingly difficult tightrope between humanitarian obligations and national self-protection. Yet as the war in the former Yugoslavia showed, peacekeeping can be an unforgiving and complex task which entails prolonged and expensive military commitments and continuing risks to those on the ground.

As we have seen, the end of World War II saw no cessation in European military activity, though most European armies suffered continuing cutbacks in both funding and manpower. Perhaps the greatest challenge they faced at the turn of the century is how to best structure and arm their forces in a climate where economy and flexibility seemed to be the watchwords for readiness. The underinvestment that prevails at the beginning of the twenty-first century, however, may well change as Europe's forces find themselves in combat zones spread around the globe, with greater and greater frequency.

▶ *This German infantryman wears a combat dress ideally suited to Europe's variable climate, wih a camouflage pattern on his jacket and helmet designed to fit temperate-zone woodland.*

Private Dutch Army Indonesia 1946

Serving only two years after Holland had been liberated from German occupation in World War II, the mixed elements of this Dutch infantryman's dress and equipment are understandable. Most prominent is the camouflage jungle suit, a two-piece uniform which was developed and used from 1943 onwards by the US during its Pacific campaigns.

The other visible item of US origin is the olive-green fatigue cap, but the helmet on top is the British Mark 1. The rest of his equipment is almost entirely of British manufacture. The webbing is the British 1937 pattern, a webbing which was the standard form for most British soldiers during World War II. Attached to the webbing is an ammunition pouch and a long bayonet scabbard for the 1907-pattern bayonet. This bayonet is fixed here to an interesting weapon: the British 9mm Lanchester submachine gun. A copy of the Bergmann MP28, this gun was exquisitely and reliably made with aesthetically attractive features such as a solid brass magazine housing. Further weaponry is worn on this soldier's right thigh in the form of a .38 Smith and Wesson revolver in a 'long' holster pouch.

From the end of World War II Dutch forces were employed in a four-year conflict to retake their colonies in the Dutch East Indies from nationalist guerrillas, but they eventually surrendered their sovereignty of the region in December 1949.

Date:	*1946*
Unit:	*Dutch Army*
Rank:	*Private*
Location:	*Indonesia*
Conflict:	*Indonesian Rebellion*

Private
Greek National Army
Northern Greece 1947

From 1946, the Greek National Army found itself fighting a vicious civil war against communist factions violently opposed to the right-wing government of Georgios Papandreou. Though the conflict was initially supported by British troops and equipment, this assistance was phased out when the UK hit a post-war economic crisis, and the Americans took over the role of sponsoring anti-communist resistance.

Acknowledging these influences, this Greek National Army soldier is kitted out in a combination of British Army clothing and an American firearm. The uniform itself consists of British Army trousers (part of the 'denims' uniform, the light working version of the combat dress), shirt, pullover and beret with web anklets over his boot-tops. The American firearm is the Thompson .45in M1A1 submachine gun, a favourite weapon of the GNA alongside Lee Enfield .303in rifles. The year 1947 saw the beginning of a GNA shift away from British equipment towards US tactics and kit. The GNA's opposition to its main opponent, the DSE, and its underground wing, YIAFAKA, was initially not very promising, as wartime conditions had left the army with little cohesion. American investment in tough training for the GNA paid off. Supported by US Helldiver bombers, the GNA conducted successful campaigns in 1949 in the Grammos mountains, taking the main communist stronghold around Mount Vitsi. The war ended in August 1949.

Date:	*1947*
Unit:	*Greek National Army*
Rank:	*Private*
Location:	*Northern Greece*
Conflict:	*Greek Civil War*

Guerrilla Greek Democratic Army 1947

In 1947, the Dimokratikos Stratos Ellados (DSE: Greek Democratic Army) was at the height of its strength. Its vigorously pursued goal was to establish a communist regime in post-war Greece. Like many guerrilla armies in the twentieth century, they dressed in whatever was at hand, while trying as much as possible to give the appearance of being a military unit.

Apart from her civilian blouse, this female DSE guerrilla freely mixes military items from the various occupying or liberating armies that Greece encountered during World War II. The battledress trousers and web anklets are from British Army combat dress, though the trousers here have been dyed black whereas the khaki colour was commonly retained. A British-style khaki side cap was also a part of many DSE uniforms. The influence of the departing German forces is apparent in the 9mm MP40 submachine gun, the standard submachine gun of the German Army and one of the greatest weapon success stories of the twentieth century. Yet there was no such thing as a standard firearm in the case of the DSE, and weapons from a whole host of nationalities and times past were put into operation.

The DSE was undone when it stepped out of the shadows of guerrilla warfare in 1948 and decided to pursue more conventional strategies of warfare. It was outnumbered and outgunned by a reinvigorated Greek National Army with US support, and forced to concede defeat.

Date:	*1947*
Unit:	*Greek Democratic Army*
Rank:	*Guerrilla*
Location:	*Greece*
Conflict:	*Greek Civil War*

Legionnaire
French Foreign Legion
Central Indochina 1952

Some 20,000 legionnaires were deployed in Indochina where their elite standards of training meant that they were destined for the toughest combat zones during France's protracted Asian war. Losses in the Legion between 1946 and 1954 were 11,620, a high percentage of the 21,000 deaths experienced by French forces in South East Asia.

As is the case with most Legion soldiers during this time, this soldier is wearing a uniform made up from a diversity of sources, both French and foreign. The combat trousers and camouflaged jacket are of US stock, the former being from the standard pattern of US fatigues, while the latter is a French adaptation of the US jacket issued to infantry combatants for the D-Day landings. The US M1 helmet with a netting cover and the US Improved M1910 web belt complete the US influences in the uniform, as the boots are the notable double-buckle type worn as standard by the Legion. An undeniably French feature of this soldier's equipment is his 9mm MAT 49 submachine gun, the ammunition being stored in the long pouch on the right hip. The MAT 49 replaced the 7.65mm MAS 38, and despite its rather boxy appearance, its 600 rounds per minute rate of fire and its folding stock made it a convenient weapon. It is still used around the world. Here the soldier supplements his firepower with two OF 37 fragmentation grenades.

Date:	*1952*
Unit:	*French Foreign Legion*
Rank:	*Legionnaire*
Location:	*Central Indochina*
Conflict:	*Indochina War*

89

Captain French Foreign Legion Indochina 1952

The 1st Foreign Legion Parachute Brigade (1 BEP) was created in June 1948 and by the November of that year was arriving for combat duties in Indochina. Along with 2 BEP, its experience in Indochina was emphatically bloody, and by the fall of Dien Bien Phu in 1954, almost all the paras had been either killed or wounded.

Many armies serving shortly after World War II were dressed and equipped from a mixture of sources. This para Captain is no exception, as the Foreign Legion in Indochina kitted itself out from French, British and US supplies. The camouflage jacket is one half of the contemporary US jungle uniform, though the trousers are from British airborne troop dress, being windproof for wear during parachute drops. Rank in this case is indicated by the patch on the front of the jacket which displays three gold bars on a blue background. Other US elements include the familiar M1 helmet, the M1910 canteen cover with black enamel water bottle, and a magazine pouch for pistol ammunition (the pistol being carried on his right hip). The rest of the webbing is a mix of French and British features, with a British 1958-pattern backpack and French braces. The firearm, though having a slightly unusual appearance at first, is the standard US .30 M1A1 carbine with a folding stock for airborne use.

The men of 1 BEP were let down, like many others, by the short-sighted French tactics that left units isolated in the midst of a motivated enemy without adequate support and backup.

Date:	*1952*
Unit:	*1 BEP*
Rank:	*Captain*
Location:	*Indochina*
Conflict:	*Indochina*

Corporal French Colonial Parachute Regt 1956

For both parties of the Anglo-French invasion force, the Suez operation was a political disaster. Despite this fact, the early airborne operations by the French, particularly the 2nd Regiment of the French Colonial Parachute Division, were an almost textbook illustration of how parachute deployment should be carried out.

The paratrooper pictured here is similar in appearance to the paras who fought in the Indochina War that had ended two years earlier than Suez. Indeed it was the presence of so many veteran soldiers that gave the French parachute operations at Suez such competence. The uniform he is wearing is the M51 parachute uniform, a uniform issued in 1953 to the paras in Indochina, which featured a bold mix of camouflage colours ranging across many shades of brown and green. It would take until 1960 until general French infantry were issued with camouflage. All his equipment, including the high-leg para boots and the basic webbing, were standard French issue, as was the 7.5mm MAS 1936 rifle which was eventually replaced in 1980 by the 5.56mm FAMAS. The French paras had an advantage over their British counterparts at Suez in that they carried their weapon for use during the actual parachute descent, whereas the British had to wait until they landed to access weapons from containers. Increasing the firepower of the rifle are the rifle grenades here seen carried in a multi-compartment pouch attached to the web belt.

Date:	*1956*
Unit:	*French Colonial Parachute Regiment*
Rank:	*Corporal*
Location:	*Port Fouad*
Conflict:	*Suez Invasion*

Guerrilla Hungary Budapest 1956

The Hungarian uprising of 1956 did not bring about its intended overthrow of the Communist government, but it did show the Soviet Union the danger of a well-motivated body of freedom fighters operating within an urban territory which they knew intimately. It was only with enormous firepower that the Soviet Union was finally able to bring the uprising under control after very heavy losses.

The one-legged fighter pictured here evokes the tenacity possessed by many Hungarian civilians during their brief resistance of communist rule. The vaguely military appearance of his outfit is created mainly by the military tunic, which is Hungarian in origin. Apart from that, his clothing is mainly from civilian stock and is made up of calf-length boots, civilian trousers and a local broad-brimmed hat. Despite such a predominance of civilian clothing, his equipment leaves no doubt as to his combative intent. On his leather Sam Browne belt is hung an ammunition pouch for a PPSH41 submachine gun, though here it carries Soviet hand-grenades. The Soviet weaponry is continued by his 7.62mm M1944 carbine, a gun which also featured a bayonet attachment which folded along the length of the muzzle, as seen here. A favourite tactic employed by the freedom fighters was to lure Soviet tanks into narrow streets, stop them by using upturned plates as fake anti-tank mines, and then destroy the vehicles by dropping molotov cocktails onto the engine compartments and pushing grenades through turret hatches and observation slits.

Date:	*1956*
Unit:	*Civilian*
Rank:	*Guerrilla*
Location:	*Budapest*
Conflict:	*Hungarian Uprising*

Private
Swedish Army (UN)
Katanga 1960

In 1960, the Belgian Congo (now Zaire) was given independence by its former colonial administrators at only a few months notice. The result was a chaotic and unstable nation which saw continual changes of government, an increasing civil violence and the UN deploying soldiers in an ultimately pointless four-year military intervention.

The Swedish army were some of the first troops to enter the Congo under UN auspices. This infantryman's UN status is clearly indicated by the blue US M1 pattern helmet and the blue arm badge, both displaying the distinctive badge of the UN: white hemisphere and laurel leaves on a blue background. The only other insignia that this soldier wears is the crossed rifles of the Swedish infantry on the green slides fixed to his shoulder straps. The overall uniform is a green drill shirt and trousers made of a lightweight and fairly loose-fitting material to suit the African climatic conditions. The green webbing has two pouches to hold the 36-round ammunition magazines for the 9mm Carl Gustav 45 submachine gun. This is actually one of the oldest submachine guns in contemporary service, still being carried by military units around the world other than the Swedish forces. Its main virtue is its solid reliability and it is here shown with its common folding stock.

Though a famously neutral country, Sweden has made significant contributions in the twentieth century under the jurisdiction of the UN, operating in such areas as Palestine, Korea, the Congo and Cyprus.

Date:	*1960*
Unit:	*Swedish Army (UN)*
Rank:	*Private*
Location:	*Katanga*
Conflict:	*Congolese Civil War*

Private French 10th Parachute Division 1961

France's military efforts to keep Algeria under French control were a prime example of meticulous, if ruthless, counter-insurgency tactics. Using local informers and vigorously executed operations, the French forces nearly reduced the nationalist ALN to breaking point, yet political movements back in their homeland resulted in Algeria's eventual independence in July 1962.

In 1957, the 10th Parachute Division and the 3rd Colonial Parachute Regiment were sent into Algeria with an open brief that allowed them to crush nationalist resistance by any means available. Operating towards the end of the conflict, this para wears the uniform of one employed on infantry-type actions rather than para drops. The uniform is standard M51 French pattern camouflage combat trousers and jacket in a lightweight tropical material (all French troops had such camouflage by 1960). The soft peaked cap probably indicates that his environment is the Algerian deserts or mountains, as this type of headgear was popular outside of the urban setting. His web belt is French made, as is his 7.5mm M1952 (AAT Mle 52) machine gun which could be used as either a light or heavy machine gun, depending on whether a bipod or tripod was selected.

The paras in Algeria were very successful, but news of their systematic torture and murder of suspects and opponents provoked an international outcry and contributed to a political nightmare for the French administration.

Date:	*1961*
Unit:	*10th Parachute Division*
Rank:	*Private*
Location:	*Near Tunisian Border*
Conflict:	*Algerian Independence War*

Warrant Officer Belgian Paracommando Stanleyville 1964

When a large number of foreign nationals were taken hostage by anti-government rebels in the Congo (Zaire) in 1964, a joint US-Belgian plan was formulated to free the hostages by military means. The US provided air transport, but generally inexperienced Belgian paracommando soldiers conducted two rapid parachute operations which freed over 2000 hostages for the loss of only three paras.

This warrant officer of the 1st Battalion, Régiment Paracommando looks almost identical to a British para of that time. The maroon beret, worn by the 1st and 3rd Battalions, is British in style and the SAS cap badge alludes to the origins of the first Belgian parachute company which operated with the SAS in World War II. Worn over a plain green T-shirt, the smock here is designed closely around the British Denison smock, and features a vivid brown, mustard-yellow and green camouflage pattern with press-stud and zip fastenings. The smock epaulettes hold this soldier's rank slides, the silver star indicating the rank of Warrant Officer and the red background with blue border being the paracommando colours.

Generally speaking, the Belgian Army in the 1960s wore British 1937-pattern equipment or, in the specific case of the paracommandos, a selection of French and British equipment. This soldier wears a 1937-pattern belt with two ammunition pouches for his 7.62mm FN-FAL rifle.

Date:	*1964*
Unit:	*1st Bn Belgian Paracommando Regiment*
Rank:	*Warrant Officer*
Location:	*Stanleyville, Congo*
Conflict:	*Congolese Civil War*

Corporal Portuguese Parachute Regiment 1970

Portugal's colonial territories were held for longer than those of most Western nations. Guinea-Bissau, Mozambique and Angola did not cede to nationalist control until the mid-1970s, and then only after protracted and costly conflict between African guerrillas and the Portuguese Army.

To meet the demands of their counter-insurgency roles, the troops employed on the ground were mainly those from the special forces such as marines and paratroopers. The paratrooper here is a corporal, his rank indicated by the light-blue chevrons fixed to his shoulder straps. Parachute regiment membership is affirmed by the winged badge on the right breast, while the beret badge is that of the Air Force, under which the paratroopers operated. The camouflage outfit is of French 1950-pattern in dark-brown, dark-green and light olive-green colours, a colour scheme which is prevalent in many African uniforms today. Personal firearms tended towards those of German manufacture, especially the popular Heckler and Koch G3 assault rifle. Extending the G3 design, the 7.62m HK21 General Purpose Machine Gun, which this soldier carries, provided a heavier belt-feed version of the G3 which could also take the standard G3 magazines.

By 1974 the Portuguese forces had lost a total of some 11,000 dead. The cost in both human life and political credibility was too high, and Portugal gave up Guinea-Bissau in 1974, with Mozambique and Angola moving to nationalist control the following year.

Date:	*1970*
Unit:	*Portuguese Parachute Regiment*
Rank:	*Corporal*
Location:	*Mozambique*
Conflict:	*African Independence Wars*

Private Turkish Army Cyprus 1974

Turkey's invasion of Cyprus in 1974 illustrated the flaws of Turkey's inadequately trained and politically partisan military. Though everything should have gone in Turkey's favour, with its supremacy of air and sea and its tactical surprise, the Turkish forces were not able to occupy more than 40 per cent of the Greek-held island.

A notable feature of the Turkish Army's equipment in the Cyprus operation was the strange diversity in its equipment, particularly its firearms. The gun this soldier is brandishing harks back to World War II: the cheaply made US .45 M3A1, here fitted with a distinctive anti-flash device on the muzzle. As this weapon was taken out of production in 1944 with a history of component failures, its value in 1974 is questionable, especially as it is meant to be part of a modern army's equipment. The US theme continues as the soldier is holding a M1 helmet with a US Marine camouflage cover and also in the M1943 webbing. Instead of the M1943's many small ammunition pouches, however, this soldier has three large Turkish-made pouches for his M3 ammunition. The overall uniform he is wearing is a simple shirt and trousers with shoulder and thigh pockets, the material being a lightweight cotton suitable for the Turkish/ Cypriot climate.

The olive-green colour used for uniforms was subsequently replaced by Disruptive Pattern Material (DPM) camouflage in the 1980s.

Date:	*1974*
Unit:	*Turkish Army*
Rank:	*Private*
Location:	*Cyprus*
Conflict:	*Invasion of Cyprus*

Corporal Royal Netherlands Marine Corps 1970s

In addition to their more orthodox military specialisms, the Royal Netherlands Marine Corps (RNMC) also boast a thoroughly competent anti-terrorist unit. It shot to fame in 1977 after a dramatic hostage rescue operation on a train captured by South Moluccan terrorists.

Extending his basic training by some 48 weeks enables a Marine to gather the requisite counter-terrorist skills, including hostage rescue, fast building entry, marksmanship and even riot control. Any specialist unit selects its firearms with care and the anti-terrorist section of the Dutch Marines tends to rely on compact submachine guns and pistols for its close-quarter operations. This Marine in the 1970s has chosen the Israeli 9mm Uzi, a gun with an almost legendary military and popular status. With a 600 rounds per minute rate of fire and a length of only 440mm (17.3in) when the stock is folded, the Uzi is an easy gun to deploy in situations where lack of space and strong firepower are the two main operating considerations. Much of the Marine's clothing is standard military issue: a heavy green pullover and olive-green trousers worn with a pair of combat boots and a US M1 helmet (rather than the black Marines beret). He wears two webbing belts around his waist and from the lower M1967 belt at the back hangs a haversack for grenades, a water bottle in a US cover and a holster for his service revolver. Apart from the Uzi, the soldier's anti-terrorist purpose is also indicated by the wearing of a flak jacket.

Date:	*1970s*
Unit:	*Royal Netherlands Marines Corps*
Rank:	*Corporal*
Location:	*Netherlands*
Conflict:	*None*

Corporal French Foreign Legion Kolwezi 1978

In 1978 a large force from the Congo National Liberation Front captured the mining town of Kolwezi in southern Zaire and reports of a massacre of European mineworkers were soon reaching Western governments. The only one to respond was the French, who sent in units from the 2nd Foreign Legion Parachute Regiment. From the start the operation was problematic, but after some hard fighting the 2REP won the town back over with the loss of only five killed and 20 wounded.

This para corporal, his rank indicated by the green chevrons attached by velcro to his chest, wears a uniform which is fully integrated with the air-drop operational requirements of the Kolwezi mission. The uniform itself is French, the 'Satin 300', an olive-green outfit designed specifically for the use of the Legion and characterised by a short, wide-collared jacket with double zip compartments and narrow trousers. From his webbing hangs a distinctive three-compartment grenade pouch (another fragmentation grenade hangs over his chest), a bayonet and two ammunition pouches (the identical bags on the right and left hips respectively). The small leather pouch on the left hip carries weapon-cleaning utensils. The French ranger boots are based, like the webbing, on US models. Though all the distinctive features of the soldier's uniform show him to be a legionnaire – especially the green Legion beret with parachute badge – he also wears a black scarf under his left shoulder strap as a further identifier.

Date:	*1978*
Unit:	*2nd French Foreign Legion Parachute Regiment*
Rank:	*Corporal*
Location:	*Kolwezi, Zaire*
Conflict:	*Kolwezi Liberation*

Mercenary Mercenary Unit 1980s

With scarcely a single day passed after World War II when conflict was not raging somewhere in the world, mercenaries rarely had trouble finding employment. Indeed, wars as recent as those in the former Yugoslavia in 1999 saw widespread mercenary participation, with former combatants of many elite fighting units offering their services for the money, their ideals or a sheer boredom with life in the civilian world.

Despite their freelance status, mercenaries often like to refer back to their previous regular military connections, if they have any. This soldier is proudly wearing his former regimental beret and badge, but apart from this, his uniform is improvised around what is available. Over a short-sleeved civilian vest he is wearing US M1956 webbing with two ammunition pouches. His trousers are of military issue, while his lightweight 'hockey' boots are a practical and comfortable form of footwear, especially when operating in hot climates such as is suggested by this mercenary's light dress. His firearm is the infamous 7.62mm FN-FAL rifle. Such has been the worldwide popularity and distribution of this firearm that it will turn up as a terrorist and mercenary weapon for many years to come.

The expanding use of mercenaries around the world by the end of the 1990s was proving to be of great concern to organisations such as the United Nations, as conflicts are often prolonged and intensified by mercenaries' professional input.

Date:	*1980s*
Unit:	*Mercenary*
Rank:	*Mercenary*
Location:	*Africa*
Conflict:	*Unknown*

Sergeant-Major Italian Folgore Brigade 1982

The 1980s saw Italy steadily increasing its Middle Eastern peacekeeping operations under the auspices of the United Nations. In 1982 over 2000 Italian marines, paras and infantry found themselves in the unenviable role of policing parts of Beirut and keeping various murderously opposed factions separate from each other and civilian/ refugee areas.

The three chevrons on this soldier's chest speak his rank as a sergeant-major and his uniform follows the classic lines of the Paracadutisti Folgore Brigade. On the collars of his jump overalls are the silver savoy stars which refer back to the birthplace of the Italian Army in the Kingdom of Sardinia-Piedmont. His jump overalls are superbly designed for parachute and combat operations. Elasticated ankles keep the shape of the trousers in the blasts of air during a parachute drop, while reinforced knee pads protect against landing damage and general wear and tear. The curiously laced parachute boots have heavy rubber soles for good adhesion on many different surfaces (including aircraft floors). His armament is the Beretta BM-59 Ital para rifle, issued to the paras on account of its folding butt and good general performance. It originated out of Beretta's manufacture under licence of the US M1 Garand rifle after the war, and Beretta took the M1 design and enhanced it for the Italian forces. This soldier is also carrying a side arm in a holster on his British 1937-pattern web belt, probably a 9mm Beretta Model 92.

Date:	*1982*
Unit:	*Folgore Brigade*
Rank:	*Sergeant-Major*
Location:	*Beirut*
Conflict:	*Lebanon War*

Legionnaire Spanish Foreign Legion 1987

The Spanish Foreign Legion retains all the mystique and austerity of its French counterpart, yet it is a uniquely Spanish force, with foreigners being excluded from its ranks entirely since 1987. A small but excellently trained force, it contains a tough brand of men who have completed a thoroughly brutal training regime before they could take their place in the Legion ranks.

The soldier is wearing a plain, everyday dress uniform common to the wider Spanish Army, though the black, buckled high boots are a specific feature of Legion dress in a similar way to those of the French Foreign Legion. Equally distinctive is the tasselled side cap, though Spanish Legion soldiers also wear a green beret pulled to the left as a regimental trademark. In combat situations, the Legion generally adopts a woodland-style camouflage combat suit with indigenous webbing systems. The leather carrying system which this soldier wears was standard Spanish Army dress during much of the 1980s though an exception to the Legion, who tended to be supplied with much more modern fabric webbing. Here the soldier carries a bayonet and ammunition for his 7.62mm CETME rifle (CETME being the company who designed the famous G3 rifle).

During the late 1980s, the 7.62 rifle was phased out in favour of a 5.56mm Model L version which accepted the smaller-sized, and now far more common, NATO cartridge.

Date:	*1987*
Unit:	*Spanish Foreign Legion*
Rank:	*Legionnaire*
Location:	*Canary Islands*
Conflict:	*None*

NCO
Belgian Parachute
Regiment 1990s

The 2nd Battalion of the Belgian Parachute Regiment is instantly distinguished by the green beret instead of the red colour worn by the 1st and 3rd Battalions. With its SAS winged-dagger badge, this cap indicates the 2nd Battalion's commando status and its attachment to the SAS during World War II.

When not wearing the beret, the Belgian paracommandos tend to don the standard NATO ballistic nylon helmet with double chin-strap and camouflaged cover and netting. In the Belgian armed forces, the paracommandos are an exception to the rule by wearing camouflage pattern uniforms as standard instead of the usual olive-drab. Paratroopers' camouflage varies from a common mix of greens and browns through to uniforms which use lighter mixes of burgundy, teal-green and khaki shades. On the jacket, rank is displayed on shoulder slides for officers and senior NCOs, or as white chevrons on the shoulder loops for NCOs. The webbing belt here appears to be based on British patterns and the soldier also carries supplies in two kidney pouches.

Belgium is home to excellent gun manufacturing firms, and this soldier holds one of the most successful modern weapons, the 7.62mm FN-MAG machine gun manufactured by Fabrique National Herstal. Its fairly rapid rate of fire (850 rounds per minute), reliability and long effective range make it a useful combat tool in a variety of roles. It has been exported widely around the world, and been adopted by a number of professional armies.

Date:	*1990s*
Unit:	*2nd Bn Belgian Parachute Regiment*
Rank:	*NCO*
Location:	*Belgium*
Conflict:	*None*

Corporal French Foreign Legion Corsica 1990s

In their combat uniform, there is little to distinguish the French Foreign Legion from many of the world's fighting units. However, in their dress uniform and classic kepi hat, their military allegiance is instantly recognisable.

On guard duty, this corporal of 2e REP wears the standard khaki Legion uniform with many additional insignia and features to describe his status and skills. The most distinctive piece of the Legion uniform is the kepi. Ordinary soldiers wear what is known as the kepi blanc which is actually a dark-coloured hat with a white cloth cover. This soldier being an NCO, he shares with officers the black uncovered kepi noir, though all hats across the ranks maintain the red top, gold badge and the chin strap (here not worn). Moving down, over the right breast is the parachute brevet which is composed of a pair of metal wings either side of a parachute emblem. As every Legion soldier is parachute trained, this badge is worn by all personnel throughout the Regiment on all uniforms, including combat dress. On the left breast, various service medals are displayed and a regimental lanyard runs under the left arm. The rest of the soldier's uniform, including the webbing belt and the footwear, is standard French Army issue.

He carries the 5.56mm FAMAS F1 rifle, the first weapon of the now-common 'bullpup' design to be adopted as a military issue. By having the firing pin close to the end of the stock, the bullpup rifle combines a long barrel with a short overall length.

Date:	*1990s*
Unit:	*French Foreign Legion*
Rank:	*Corporal*
Location:	*Corsica*
Conflict:	*None*

Operative French GIGN France 1990s

The *Groupe d'Intervention Gendarmarie Nationale* (GIGN) came to public attention when Air France flight 8969 was taken over by four militant Algerian guerrillas on 24 December 1994 at Algiers Houari-Boumedienne International airport. By 1735 hours on 26 December all the guerrillas were dead, killed by the GIGN in a dramatic – and televised – plane assault on the airport tarmac at Marseilles.

GIGN was formed in 1974 as a fast response force to counter the efforts of the many terrorist forces aligned against France in the 1970s. Vital to the success of many of their operations have been the talents of GIGN snipers such as the one pictured here. His overall appearance testifies to the excellent quality of GIGN combat materials. He is wearing the specially designed GIGN sniper coverall, though the addition of a pair of thermal-imaging goggles with built-in communication mike means that the standard-issue black balaclava has been omitted. Like most GIGN operatives, over his right breast he wears his parachutist wings. Attached to his waistbelt is a radio set and an abseiling rope and harness, essential for reaching the best vantage points in a hostage situation. His sniper rifle is the French 7.62mm Giat FR-F2, a tried and tested precision weapon. As a sniper, his combat uniform differs somewhat from that of assault troops, who generally wear the GIGN's characteristic blue overalls with an assault vest to carry ammunition and a Kevlar helmet with visor.

Date:	*1990s*
Unit:	*GIGN*
Rank:	*Operative*
Location:	*France*
Conflict:	*None*

Operative German GSG-9 Anti-Terrorist Unit 1990s

The GSG-9 anti-terrorist squad was born out of the tragedy that occurred in Munich in 1972, when an inefficient attempt by German police to free the Israeli Olympic team hostages from their Arab terrorist captors resulted in nine of the Israeli athletes being killed, in addition to the two who were killed at the start of the Arab action.

To avoid the terrible errors committed in this operation ever happening again, the German Government established *Grenzschutzgruppe-9* (GSG-9), now regarded and proved as one of the world's foremost anti-terrorist groups. The high investment that GSG-9 attracts from the German Government means that uniforms and equipment are first rate, though like all counter-terrorist units, there is no such thing as a standard set of clothing. The soldier here is very much geared up for an airborne deployment, most likely from a helicopter, as he is wearing a black para-style helmet and an airborne harness over his uniform. Face and hands are covered with, respectively, a black balaclava and close-fitting gloves and a radio is secured to his left shoulder for ease of communications. Though there is no standard uniform, the GSG-9 operators commonly wear sage-green coveralls and a close-fitting load-bearing system when operational. A camouflage helmet more like the US PASGT helmet is generally worn. The gun he holds, the 9mm Heckler and Koch MP5A3, is the GSG-9 favourite, respected as an accurate rapid-fire weapon with real stopping power.

Date:	*1990s*
Unit:	*Grenzschutzgruppe-9*
Rank:	*Anti-Terrorist Operative*
Location:	*Germany*
Conflict:	*None*

Private
Italian Alpini
North Italy 1990s

The trademark of the Alpini soldier, not worn in this particular case, is the grey-green felt mountaineer's cap with a black eagle feather and pompom and a cap badge which shows an eagle above an infantry bugle with regimental number. The feather is worn with all forms of headgear, including helmets, though this Alpini is dressed without ceremonial features in a straightforward combat uniform.

The Alpini are separated into five brigades: Tidentina; Orobica; Iuwa; Cadore; and Tauninense. Regardless of the Brigade, all Alpini soldiers are experts in climbing and winter warfare skills, including excellent abilities in cross-country skiing. The corresponding winter uniform is a white hooded jacket and trousers with gloves and boots suited to sub-zero conditions. The soldier here, however, wears an Italian-issue camouflage uniform with built-in knee and elbow pads, and calf-length combat/climbing boots. On his back hangs a sleeping bag and a small rucksack, with kit weight kept to a minimum for the demands of scaling difficult terrain. The silver savoy stars on the collar are worn throughout the Italian Army, though Alpini also wear green collar patches. The weapon carried here, the Beretta 7.62mm BM59 Alpini rifle, has features which make it ideal for use by the Alpini. These include a folding stock for enhanced portability and a special trigger to use when wearing ski gloves. In much of the Italian Army, the BM59 has now been replaced by the .223 Beretta AR70.

Date:	*1990s*
Unit:	*Italian Alpini*
Rank:	*Private*
Location:	*North Italy*
Conflict:	*None*

Police Officer Italian NOCS Milan 1990s

NOCS is the abbreviation of *Nucleo Operativo Centrale*. **Made up of some 100 operatives, it forms the counter-terrorist and hostage rescue unit for the Italian State Police. Being part of the national police means that its duties extend to tackling dangerous armed criminals as well as terrorist forces, and it has proved its worth as an operational unit.**

The only item of dress that would distinguish this man from any other counter-terrorist operative is the police shield on the right shoulder. In every other way he is wearing 'standard' urban special forces clothing consisting of black overalls and a protective helmet with a face visor. An additional – and potentially lifesaving – piece of clothing is the Kevlar flak jacket which has the capability to stop most small arms rounds, even at close range. The expertise of the NOCS operatives is suggested by the fast-roping kit worn on the belt here, the trooper being able to use a nylon climbing rope and harness to lower himself rapidly from any vantage spot. Once there he is able to deploy his firepower, and in this case the policeman has chosen two standard Italian weapons, both made by Beretta.

The submachine gun is the 9mm Beretta Model 12S, a weapon which first entered service with the Italian Army as the Model 12 in 1961, and has remained in use by the armed forces by being updated with a number of improvements. The handgun holstered on the police officer's belt is the 9mm Beretta Model 84.

Date:	*1990s*
Unit:	*Nucleo Operativo Centrale*
Rank:	*Police Officer*
Location:	*Milan*
Conflict:	*None*

Private Italian Folgore Brigade 1990s

Italy has a long tradition of pioneering the parachute as a vehicle for the rapid deployment of a military force. The most distinctive Italian parachute unit is the Folgore Brigade, formed in 1942 and thereafter finding extensive post-war service with NATO and UN forces.

Like most paratroopers around the world, the soldiers of the Folgore Brigade wear a maroon beret which displays their parachute wings, though the soldier here has a standard parachute helmet with cover and chinstrap. The uniform of the soldier here is not the typical green, brown and sand camouflage worn by Italian parachute soldiers, whose jackets and trousers often have reinforced elbow- and knee-patches respectively. This para is instead wearing a plain uniform that does not have the elasticated wrists and ankles which feature on the camouflage outfit. Distinguishing insignia of the Folgore Brigade is the parachute wings on the right breast and the silver savoy stars on the collar tabs. The colour of the background of the parachute badge defines the soldier's function within the Brigade, with all members of the Brigade except specialists displaying a blue background.

Two other features define this soldier's status as a paratrooper. The first is his brown combat boots (instead of the usual Italian Army black) and the firearm: the 7.62mm BM-59 rifle with a folding stock is the para version of the Italian Army's standard service rifle.

Date:	*1990s*
Unit:	*Folgore Brigade*
Rank:	*Private*
Location:	*Central Italy*
Conflict:	*None*

109

Marine Italian San Marco Battalion 1990s

The San Marco Battalion is an elite part of the Italian Marines. All San Marco marines complete an exacting training course at the Military Paratroop School in Pisa and gain versatile skills in amphibious, coastal and airborne assault plus a variety of other specialist roles.

The soldier here is notable for his white winter smock and soft cap, indicative of the many theatres of operation which the San Marco Battalion has to encompass as part of ongoing national, NATO and UN commitments. The smock covers the woodland-style patterning of Italian army camouflage, a camouflage that mixes olive-green with browns of ochre and clay shades. San Marco uniforms cross army and navy alliances, for the Marines wear the combat uniform of the Army but the parade uniform of the Navy. In non-combat dress, all ranks bear the insignia of the San Marco: a golden winged lion on a red background. This insignia is worn on the collar and right sleeve cuff. However, the soldier here has a complete absence of visible insignia. His boots are a mix of leather sole and canvas uppers, which allow a high degree of 'breathability'. The firearm is the 7.92mm MG42/59 which is a standard weapon in the Italian and Austrian armies. The most exceptional San Marco Marines can go on to a 10-week course run by COMSUBIN (the naval special forces), after which they become members of the elite Italian incursion group, the *Demolitori Ostacoli Antisbarco*, or Shore Demolition Unit.

Date:	*1990s*
Unit:	*San Marco Battalion*
Rank:	*Marine*
Location:	*North Italy*
Conflict:	*None*

Officer
Spanish GEO
Madrid 1990s

The *Grupo Especial de Operaciones* (GEO) is Spain's foremost counter-terrorist group with a particular speciality in hostage rescue. Their elite capabilities against terrorism are far from theo-retical, as their ongoing fight in Spain against the Basque separatist organ-isation ETA has given them more direct operational experience than most other similar units around the world.

Like all elite forces, the GEO selects its uniform and equipment according to operational requirements. However, rather than the black overalls commonly worn by counter-terrorist units, the GEO tends to wear Spanish-made leaf/forest-pattern camouflage trousers and shirt and the footwear of choice. The soldier pictured here repeats this uniform with the addition of a full-face balaclava which not only prevents disclosure of the soldier's identity but also makes him a harder target in the confusion and smoke of a hostage-taking situation. Personal weaponry of the GEO combatant is usually the Heckler and Koch 9mm MP5A2 submachine gun (usually, as here, fitted with a shoulder sling) and the Heckler and Koch P-9S 9mm semi-automatic pistol worn on the waist. Here this soldier has taped together two magazines for his MP5A2 to facilitate rapid reloading in combat. Naturally, the appearance and firearms of the GEO change dramatically with the mission at hand, for in addition to hostage-taking sections, the GEO also has a maritime counter-terrorist group and an airborne-qualified section.

Date:	1990s
Unit:	Grupo Especial de Operaciones
Rank:	Counter-Terrorist Officer
Location:	Madrid
Conflict:	None

Marine
Royal Netherlands
Marine Corps 1980s

The Royal Netherlands Marine Corps (RNLMC) is the Netherlands' oldest military unit with a history dating back to 1665. The specialities within the Dutch Marines are diverse, and apart from amphibious assault capabilities, include counter-terrorist and parachute expertise.

This Marine is wearing standard unit dress of the 1980s consisting of an olive-green field uniform which, though similar to the uniform of other Dutch soldiers, has a different colour and cut from the regular style. Marines are also supplied with a stone-coloured shirt and a heavy ribbed green jumper, and if these are not worn on their own, they are covered with a combat jacket which is the same colour as the trousers. A departure from this was the uniform of Whisky company which, because of its attachment to the British 3 Commando Brigade, wore British camouflage clothing, though today the Marines in general have their own or British DPM camouflage pattern. Regarding footwear, the Marines tend to wear black combat boots rather than the brown ones worn by other Dutch military units. Insignia on the Marines uniform is very limited, with the rank usually being displayed on shoulder slides.

This private is evidently on exercise, with his US-style helmet completely obscured by attached foliage. Like most Marine units around the world, regimental berets are a signature of pride and are often worn instead of helmets. The Dutch Marine beret is black with an anchor badge positioned on a red background.

Date:	*1980s*
Unit:	*Royal Netherlands Marine Corps*
Rank:	*Private*
Location:	*Netherlands*
Conflict:	*None*

Private
1st Airborne Division
West Germany 1985

Ready for a static-line parachute jump, this *Fallschirmjäger* **(as German paratroopers are known) of the 1st Airborne Division wears a typical uniform for the mid-1980s. Though the German paratroopers, like paras almost everywhere around the world, like to wear distinguishing red berets (the German berets displaying a diving eagle cap badge), for actual jumps it is obviously safer to wear the protective para helmet.**

It is most likely that the soldier pictured here is on a training jump, as in combat situations the helmet would usually be camouflaged by a cloth cover made from old poncho material or netting. In addition, no gun or webbing is carried, just his main chute at the back and his reserve chute at the front of his chest with the metal-handled ripcord clearly visible on the right of the pack. Before it was generally replaced by a modern camouflage combat dress, the uniform of the airborne soldiers was a standard field grey and featured close fitting trousers which were tucked tightly into the boots to avoid snagging upon landing. The boots themselves are parachute issue, going very high up the leg to reduce the risk of sprained ankles, and cross-laced for a very strong fit. Just visible on the soldier's left sleeve is a small cloth badge giving the colours of the German Federal Republic.

A distinct group within the division are the *Fallschirmpanzerabwehr* companies. These specialise in the rapid deployment of anti-tank weaponry, such as the TOW AT missile.

Date:	1985
Unit:	1st Airborne Division
Rank:	Private
Location:	West Germany
Conflict:	None

113

Israel

Israel's unique history as a nation under siege has led it to develop one of the world's most professional and combat-tested armies. The informality that often creeps into the dress of Israeli soldiers belies the superior standards of discipline and equipment that Israel has utilised in many conflicts since her foundation in 1948.

Israel

If we were to look for a conflict which exemplified the quality of the Israeli armed forces, the Six-Day War would be the most fitting. The Six-Day War was in every sense a conventional campaign, an attempt by Israel to make a pre-emptive strike against its hostile Arab neighbours and to secure wider territorial buffer zones between it and its opponents. What makes it notable is the strategic excellence and the formidable daring which the Six-Day War displayed, a short conflict that showed all the reasons why Israel has produced one of the most successful battle-tested military forces in the world.

Israel had been at war with its Arab neighbours since the very first day of its existence on 14 May 1948, when Syria, Egypt, Iraq, Lebanon and Transjordan assaulted en masse in an attempt to strangle the Jewish state at birth. Yet Israel fought back and produced a remarkable victory over the huge combined forces of these five Arab nations despite deficiencies in manpower and weaponry. Sheer courage and tactical daring helped bring success, and these were to be tested again in the Suez War in 1956. However, by 1967 Israel recognised that it did not have the economic muscle to conduct long campaigns, and when Israeli/Arab relations further deteriorated in that year, Israel decided to go on the offensive with an explosive strategy.

On 5 June 1967, Israel launched blitzkrieg-style air attacks on Egypt, Jordan, Syria and Iraq before committing fast-moving and heavy armoured assaults into Sinai, the Golan Heights and West Jordan. The tactic of rapidly deploying air- and land-based firepower proved irresistible, as air supremacy was quickly asserted (the opponents lost almost their entire air forces in the initial strike) which in turn provided a more permissive environment in which armour could operate. In only six days the Israelis had captured all of Sinai, the Golan Heights and all Jordanian territory west of the River Jordan, including Jerusalem.

False Security

The Six-Day War was a landmark victory for the Israeli Defence Force (IDF) because it demonstrated the full maturity that its equipment and tactics has reached. By 1967, the IDF had access to a potential 260,000 personnel through Israel's 'nation-in-arms' policy, which trained all fit Israeli citizens in military skills. This bred a distinctly military-orientated society which, combined with the latest US and British weaponry, made for an extremely capable army.

However, the Six-Day War probably made Israel a victim of its own success. Because of the significance of airpower and armoured assault in 1967, much of the IDF's strategic mentality shifted towards an over-reliance on these elements, even though the Six-Day War saw very heavy fighting between ground troops. In 1973, the armies of Egypt and Syria went on the offensive against Israel in what was to be known as the Yom Kippur War. Egypt, now aware of Israel's tactical qualities, moved rapidly across the Suez canal into Sinai. Instead of advancing to meet Israel in a conventional battle, a battle which would have favoured Israel's mobility, the Egyptian forces set up positions around which they threw a defensive shield of new surface-to-air missile systems and anti-tank rockets. Its strategy was to allow the Israeli forces to wear themselves down on this shield, and it worked. IDF losses of both tanks and aircraft were extremely heavy. The only thing that saved them from defeat was when Syria found itself outgunned in the Golan Heights, and Egypt, in an attempt to relieve the Syrian situation, advanced further into Sinai and fell foul of the Israeli abilities they had avoided in the first place. Following this conflict, Israel made sure that its ground forces would always receive proper investment and tactical roles.

The almost ceaseless conflict in which Israel has found itself since its formation produced a deeply experienced military force with an enviable range of military skills. The two conflicts described above were very much conventional battles, but Israel also fought many other types of operation, from strategic artillery duels to counter-terrorist missions. Counter-terrorist operations in particular deserve a special mention, as the IDF contains within its ranks some of the world's most elite special forces whose skills have been tested in seemingly impossible missions rather than remaining in theory.

Many of the IDF's regular army units – the Golani Brigade or the Paras, for instance – have elite capabilities or sub-units, but perhaps the most famed of Israel's special forces is the Sayeret Mat'kal, or General Staff Reconnaissance Unit. Formed in 1957, the abilities and nerve of this counter-terrorist unit almost beggar belief. They have specialised in operations deep within enemy territory, usually working under cover on assassination or surveillance duties. Their list of achievements would fill a book in itself and included attacks on PLO headquarters and personnel and some of the most memorable hostage rescues in the history of counter-terrorism. However, their very ruthlessness tended to act as a magnet for international condemnation.

Culture and War

The Sayeret Mat'kal are worth mentioning because they illustrate the heights of Israel's generally superb military resources. Israel is a sophisticated country, a cultured place where a vivid history, faith and ethnic mix produce an intelligence and vibrancy that attracts worldwide tourism. Yet her very survival has depended upon the IDF, and in many ways she was as much a warrior nation in the last century as it was in the time of Abraham or Joshua.

Israel continually invests in the best military technology, particularly that of the US and the UK, so its soldiers tend to be well equipped. The dress code of the Israeli soldier often wanders towards the informal, though the basic dress is the standard olive-green fatigues with broad-strap webbing and a ballistic nylon helmet. The prevalent tendency to make personal adaptations to this uniform does not indicate a lack of discipline amongst IDF soldiers: the IDF has never lacked operational order or self-control. Rather it is perhaps indicative of an army that works under genuine threat rather than theoretical risk, an army where discipline is assured because lives depend on it and standards of dress come somewhat further down the list of priorities.

Since the Yom Kippur War, Israel has never ceased in military activity. Events such as ongoing counter-terrorism operations, an invasion of the Lebanon in 1982, and retaliatory air and rocket attacks against the Lebanese Hezbollah organisation, kept Israel's combatants at a state of readiness. A year rarely went by in which the IDF was not committed to active service, though with various peace initiatives in progress, we wait to see what the twenty-first century will mean for this strong, yet isolated, nation.

◄ *Though he wears a T-shirt instead of his fatigue jacket, this Israeli soldier illustrates the dangers of patrol duties in the Gaza Strip by his choice of a heavy flak jacket.*

▼ *The Israeli soldier has a greater likelihood of facing combat than most other soldiers in the world, and so carries the firepower to meet every eventuality, such as this ex-Soviet RPG launcher.*

Irregular Palmach Infantry Palestine 1948

The Israeli nation was born from war. With the UN's proposed partition of Palestine into Jewish and Arab territories in November 1947 came a surge in violence between various opposing irregular forces. On the Jewish side were the Haganah, a well-organised defence force which included the more experienced Palmach infantry.

Faced with all the problems in equipping itself which you would expect in a fledgling nation, the Haganah were to be seen in a mix of army surplus from around the world and had the general appearance of World War II troops. Though he presents a fairly consistent appearance, this Palmach soldier's uniform is patched together from various sources, with his khaki drill shirt being of US origin and his drill trousers being from the British Army. Footwear and headgear are both of a civilian source and a splash of colour is added to the uniform by the red-and-white shemagh scarf worn around his neck, a type of scarf worn by many military units throughout the Middle East.

In terms of equipment, this soldier wears a US Army cartridge belt dating back to World War I, while his water canteen and M1910 cover have the same national source but date from World War II and are probably US surplus. The firearm is the 7.92mm Model 24 rifle, which was a Czech version of the German Kar 98k carbine used by the Wehrmacht in World War II, and this soldier has a Model 24 bayonet fitted in a British bayonet frog.

Date:	*1948*
Unit:	*Palmach Infantry*
Rank:	*Irregular*
Location:	*Palestine*
Conflict:	*Israel's Wars of Independence*

Private
Sayeret Golani
Mount Hermon 1967

After a soldier has served six months in the regular Golani Brigade, he is able to apply for a transfer to the Brigade's elite reconnaissance unit, the Sayeret Golani. Formed in 1951, the Sayeret Golani demand another one year and eight months of training before a soldier is deemed to have the top-level surveillance, combat, counter-terrorism, parachuting and other specialist skills for this versatile and tested fighting force.

Most Sayeret Golani soldiers wear the standard olive-green IDF uniform, yet this soldier is wearing a lizard-pattern camouflage combat dress which was popular with many elite Israeli units when on conventional combat duties. Over this uniform he is wearing the Israeli-produced 'battledress' jacket: a substantial zippered jacket which also came in a fur collar variety. The helmet, a British issue airborne helmet covered with camouflage netting, deviates entirely from Israeli products, as the Sayeret Golani could choose their combat uniforms with a high degree of licence. The webbing is, typically for the time, an Israeli version of US webbing patterns. Around the soldier's neck are looped two belts of 7.62mm ammunition. These are for the heavy barrelled FN-FAL support weapon, a more substantial version of the standard Israeli firearm (though the FN series was replaced in Israel by the Galil after 1967).

During the Six-Day War, the Sayeret Golani's most significant action was its capture of the Syrian-held Mount Hermon, a job it performed again in 1973.

Date:	*1967*
Unit:	*Sayeret Golani*
Rank:	*Private*
Location:	*Mount Hermon*
Conflict:	*Six-Day War*

Private
Israeli Defence Force
Jerusalem 1967

Though it was to be Israel's use of air and armour forces that would provide the defining memory of the Six-Day War, there was much hard fighting on the ground between Israeli troops and their Arab opponents. Indeed, the lack of acknowledgement of the foot soldiers' role in this conflict led to an over-reliance on mechanisation for which the Israelis paid dearly in the Yom Kippur War.

By 1967, the Israeli Defence Force (IDF) was very well equipped and took its stocks from a variety of international suppliers. The uniform and equipment of the infantryman pictured here is thoroughly eclectic and comes from French, US and Belgian sources as well as the native Israel. The clothing itself is a mix of French paratroop trousers rendered in jungle camouflage and a woollen shirt, probably made locally. Headgear is the US M1 steel helmet covered with a camouflage net and secured by a large rubber band. In terms of equipment carried, the webbing belt and straps appear to be based on the British 1944-pattern system, while the ammunition pouches are of the British 1958 pattern. These pouches would be custom-made for the magazines of the 7.62mm FN-FAL rifle, which was standard issue for many armies around the world at this time, including the British Army and the IDF (the rifle here is an Israeli version of the FN). Yet all the webbing is Israeli-produced, even the water-bottle container so clearly designed around the US M1956-pattern carrier.

Date:	*1967*
Unit:	*Israeli Defence Force*
Rank:	*Private*
Location:	*Jerusalem*
Conflict:	*Six-Day War*

First Lieutenant Israeli Armoured Corps 1967

The combination of devastating air power and the brilliant tactical use of armour made the Six-Day War a consummate success for Israel. The 800 tanks available to Israel by 1967 were mainly British Centurions and US M4s and M48s, all tanks with excellent battlefield handling and firepower.

A central priority within a modern Main Battle Tank (MBT) is communication between crew members, vehicles and headquarters. This Israeli tank commander's helmet contains the necessary communication tools, with a foldable boom microphone in front of his mouth and receivers in the ear pieces. The junction box for the communication system hangs around his neck. The helmet itself is based on a US World War II model and is made of fibre and leather. Its padded earpieces and protective dome provided head safety, while the ventilation holes were welcome in the hot interior of a tank in action.

The commander's rank is presented by the two khaki bars on a khaki slide on the shoulder straps of the olive-green uniform. As he would be operating inside a cramped armoured vehicle, web belt equipment is minimal, but it includes a service revolver, a small ammunition pack and a water bottle. Uniforms in the Israeli armed forces are often inconsistent in their features between individuals, partly because of civilian influences in this particularly military society. In 1965, clothing regulations were tightened in the armoured corps to give a more standardised appearance.

Date:	*1967*
Unit:	*Israeli Armoured Corps*
Rank:	*First Lieutenant*
Location:	*Sinai*
Conflict:	*Six-Day War*

Private
Golani Brigade
Golan Heights 1967

The Six-Day War was defined by Israel's strong use of airpower and armoured assault, yet this short conflict also saw intense fighting between ground troops. Troops of the elite Golani Brigade were at the forefront of the clashes between Israeli and Arab forces and on the Golan Heights they were responsible for taking out 13 enemy positions.

This Golani Private is carrying the 9mm Uzi submachine gun, truly one of the most famous weapons this century, with a name that has even extended itself into popular vocabulary. The advantages of the Uzi for this soldier are its compact dimensions, its light weight (especially welcome in the long-running battles of the Six-Day War) and a high rate of fire (600 rounds per minute). As an Israeli-produced weapon, this Uzi is one of the few pieces of indigenous equipment that this soldier is carrying, for his uniform is from a variety of sources. The rippled battledress is of French origin, and is worn over a thin open-neck jumper.

His head is protected by the US M1 helmet with a camouflaged netting cover, a ubiquitous piece of headgear in service with many armies after World War II, and a precursor to the lighter ballistic nylon helmets worn by Israeli forces today. As well as the Uzi, the webbing is another exception to the mostly foreign sources of equipment, being of native Israeli manufacture. This particular example supports two ammunition pouches, a water bottle and other combat-essential equipment.

Date:	*1967*
Unit:	*Golani Brigade*
Rank:	*Private*
Location:	*Golan Heights*
Conflict:	*Six-Day War*

Crewman
Aeromedical Evacuation
Unit 1973

Jumping to ground from his helicopter, this crewman of Unit 669 Aeromedical Evacuation Unit (AEU) would have been a welcome sight to many of the injured Israeli soldiers during the Yom Kippur war. The AEU personnel are trained, however, not only in emergency medical procedures, but also in a wide range of combat skills that enable them to operate in acutely dangerous fighting environments.

This soldier is wearing an Israeli-copy of the US K2B flight suit (the US originals were also commonly worn by the Israelis), which was a one-piece olive-green overall with large capacity zippered pockets on both chest and legs. Apart from a US web belt, no load-carrying equipment is here worn, though operational Israeli aircrew would often be seen wearing a variety of survival pouches which contained basic first aid, communications, and navigation equipment. Another popular addition was a 9mm Beretta M1951 for personnel protection. As well as the K2B suit, the boots and helmet also belong to airborne life. The boots are Israeli-made black pilot boots with rubber soles and the helmet is the US Army's CVC 'bone dome' with a boom-mike attachment. This helmet was not only worn by Israeli forces but by many other Middle Eastern armies as well, other popular helmets including the single-visored HGU-26 and SPH-4C.

The crewman probably flies within a Bell 212 helicopter, an adaptable flying machine used in both medevac and assault roles.

Date:	*1973*
Unit:	*Unit 669 Aeromedical Evac Unit*
Rank:	*Crewman*
Location:	*Sinai*
Conflict:	*Yom Kippur War*

Corporal 202nd Parachute Brigade 1982

The Israeli paras in the 1980s were active in the Lebanon in both patrol and counter-terrorism roles. Their mix of battle-tested combat skills and versatile training made them ideal for attacking centres of PLO resistance in Southern Lebanon.

This parachute corporal is equipped for maximum personal firepower. His firearm is the Israeli 5.56mm Galil assault rifle, here seen with its butt in the folded position. The Galil was developed to be a superior firearm by the Israeli defence industry, and its popularity has extended beyond the Israeli Defence Force (IDF) to many other armies across the world. The pouches worn at the front of the soldier's body are for the Galil's 35- or 50-round magazines, and the webbing in general is standard Israeli issue, recognisable by its broad shoulder straps and lace belt-connectors. The clearly visible fins protruding from the para's backpack belong to the IMI bullet-trap rifle grenade. Fired directly from the muzzle of the Galil, these add an extra dimension of operational firepower in the fluid situations of anti-terrorist roles, though the 40mm M203 integral grenade launcher is often preferred for its practicality and convenience (an example of which can be seen on page 128).

The rest of the soldier's uniform is standard Israeli combat dress: olive-green shirt and trousers tucked into brown combat boots, yet the helmet is the ballistic nylon para helmet which replaced the use of steel helmets. On his left arm are the two white bars which indicate the rank of corporal.

Date:	*1982*
Unit:	*202nd Parachute Brigade*
Rank:	*Corporal*
Location:	*South Lebanon*
Conflict:	*Israeli Invasion of Lebanon*

First Lieutenant Sayeret Tzanhanim Lebanon 1985

The Sayeret Tzanhanim are another elite unit within the Israeli Defence Force (IDF), this one being the reconnaissance unit for the parachute brigade. Like all reconnaissance units, their standards of training are exceptionally high, and this training found its active expression during combat patrol duties in the Lebanon in the 1980s.

The two black bars on this soldier's shoulder slides indicate that he is a Segen, or 1st Lieutenant. His appearance at first seems rather odd for a combat paratrooper, as his uniform is based around the winter climate of the Lebanon and the armoured method of deployment. The uniform itself is the Beged Horef, a one-piece suit issued for winter use on account of its thick, insulated material. Here it is worn on its own, though it was much more common for soldiers to wear it under other uniform items, especially an Israeli-issue rainproof jacket which added waterproofing to warmth. The reconnaissance forces in the Lebanon were usually deployed from the globally popular M113 APC (Armoured Personnel Carrier), hence this soldier's Type 602 armoured crewman's protective helmet. This helmet, which was based around US designs and contained internal communications equipment, was made of Kevlar and replaced the earlier ballistic nylon version. Held down by this soldier's side is the standard Israeli firearm, the 5.56mm Galil assault rifle. Other popular firearms for the reconnaissance troops included the 9mm Uzi submachine gun and the US M16A2 assault rifle.

Date:	*1985*
Unit:	*Sayeret Tzanhanim*
Rank:	*First Lieutenant*
Location:	*Lebanon*
Conflict:	*Arab / Israeli Wars*

Private Golani Infantry Brigade 1990s

As the only unit in the Israeli Defence force (IDF) with a regular army status, the Golani Infantry has had more combat experience than any other unit of Israel's forces. The Golani's impressive counter-terrorist and armoured deployment skills have been used to incisive effect wherever Israel has needed a capable rapid-reaction force or an incisive battlefield presence.

The absence of headgear on this particular Golani infantryman is not unusual, as the IDF often exhibits an informality of dress in operational circumstances, though a brown beret is sometimes worn by those soldiers who have successfully completed their training (along with the usual selection of protective helmets). As a warranted medical precaution, operational headgear often has the individual wearer's bloodgroup marked on the side. When not in combat dress, the Golani soldiers have a parade dress which consists of the brown beret with an olive-coloured service shirt and paratroop trousers. Yet whatever uniform they don, the Golani often wear a distinctive tunic pin on the left breast pocket flap: a horizontal knife on which a figurative tree is superimposed, this combined image sitting on a red background. When wearing their webbing, troops often keep the six main pouches positioned to the front for more rapid access to ammunition, while water bottles are worn to the rear. Typically, this soldier carries the 5.56mm Galil assault rifle.

Date:	*1990s*
Unit:	*Golani Infantry Brigade*
Rank:	*Private*
Location:	*Lebanese Border*
Conflict:	*Arab / Israeli*

Private
Israeli Defence Force
Gaza Strip 1990s

The politics of Israel have kept the Israeli Defence Force (IDF) in a constant state of combat involvement. Throughout the 1990s, contested territories such as the Gaza Strip required regular patrolling by Israeli soldiers, patrols which were frequently dangerous and stressful for those on the ground.

This soldier here is most likely deployed in a covering role, protecting patrol members or vehicles using the firepower of a 5.56mm Galil rifle when fitted with a grenade-firing attachment. The IMI bullet-trap rifle grenades here used can be fired with any type of 5.56mm ammunition and fit directly onto the muzzle of the Galil. Each grenade comes with a large plastic sight, here visible on the top of the rifle just behind the fins of the loaded grenade, a sight which is thrown away after each shot. A variety of charges can be unleashed by these grenades, including Armour Piercing (AP), High Explosive (HE), Smoke and Illumination.

The soldier's uniform is standard Israeli issue: a ballistic nylon combat helmet, olive-green trousers and shirt, standard webbing and flak jacket, the latter a wise precautionary item in the unpredictable street-patrol conditions these soldiers faced. One interesting feature is the Na'alei Kommando boots. Made from tan canvas with thick, reinforced soles, they are not standard issue but provide a comfortable option to the usual army footwear.

Date:	*1990s*
Unit:	*Israeli Defence Force*
Rank:	*Private*
Location:	*Gaza Strip*
Conflict:	*Arab / Israeli*

Private 202nd Parachute Brigade 1990s

The paratroopers of the Israeli Army had their origins back in May 1948 during Israel's independence war, but they were regularised into the 202nd Parachute Brigade in 1955. Since then the 202nd has fought in all Israel's major conflicts, and conducted daring counter-terrorist operations such as the attack on the PLO headquarters in 1968 and the hostage-rescue actions at Lod Airport in 1972 and Entebbe in 1976.

The uniforms of Israeli paratroopers, like most Israeli military outfits, can lack consistency in operational conditions, when a certain informality creeps in (though not into their combat abilities). However, the soldier pictured here wears the typical Israeli Army uniform. Over the olive drab uniform is worn the Israeli issue webbing, easily defined by its broad shoulder straps and lace connectors. Kevlar flak jackets are usually worn as an important level of protection on operational and patrol duties. The ballistic-nylon helmet is a common piece of Israeli Army headgear, though the paras often replace this with the regimental red beret. This beret is awarded to the soldier only after five successful static-line parachute jumps. Other insignia can include a silver parachute-wings badge worn over the left breast. This soldier's firearm is the US M16A1 in contrast to the Galil assault rifle. Attached below the barrel is the M203 grenade launcher which can fire 40mm grenades containing a variety of charges such as fragmentation, smoke, and shotgun.

Date:	*1990s*
Unit:	*202nd Parachute Brigade*
Rank:	*Private*
Location:	*Gaza Strip*
Conflict:	*Arab/Israeli*

The Middle East

The Middle East has been one of the most violent world regions since World War II. Arab-Israeli and inter-Arab tensions have led to conflicts ranging from small scale terrorist acts to prodigious conventional wars, with huge losses in both military and civilian lives, and the use of ever more destructive weaponry.

▲ *This Syrian infantryman illustrates the fact that what many Middle Eastern soldiers lack in sophisticated equipment, they make up for with a plentiful supply of basic clothing and weaponry.*

Since 1945, few regions in the world have seen as much conflict as the Middle East. Even as the last echoes of World War II were still reverberating across the globe, new shots were being heard in the region as its complex religious, political and territorial tensions boiled over into war.

There were many influences involved in the Middle East's wars, but as a general division they tended to fall into three categories: wars between Arab nations and Israel, inter-Arab wars, and wars which brought outside nations into the Middle East itself. Of all the causes of instability, it is the first category that engendered more ongoing strife than any of the others. On 14 May 1948, the Jewish homeland of Israel was created and immediately plunged into war as the combined forces of Syria, Egypt, Iraq, Lebanon and Transjordan went all out to destroy the new nation at birth, supported by large numbers of Palestinian Arabs. Amazingly, Israel overcame the attacks from all directions and survived, but at the end of the twentieth century, the tensions and wars continued with significant territorial shifts and a heavy bloodshed.

Perhaps the most telling aspect of the Arab/Israel conflicts was the general supremacy of Israeli forces over those of the Arab nations. The Six-Day War in 1967, for instance, saw Israel's application of Blitzkrieg-type tactics, resulting in a prodigious defeat for Egyptian, Jordanian and Syrian forces, and large territorial gains for Israel. The scale of the Arab defeat was in part due to the brilliance of Israel's action, but it also hinged on the Arabs' outdated tactics, which were often based on Soviet theories of mass warfare. In 1972, the new president of Egypt, Anwar Sadat, made a break from the Soviet Union, and in 1973 the Yom Kippur War showed a new side to the Arab armies. Egypt executed a lightning air and armour assault across the Suez Canal, while in the north Syria came close to recapturing the Golan Heights. These attacks saw Arab forces applying air and ground defence technology more successfully, and their new boldness took them close to victory. However, the problems of coordinating inter-Arab armies – problems which have since dogged many Arab actions against Israel – raised their head and once again the Arab soldiers were defeated by the highly adaptable Israeli forces.

After the Yom Kippur War, the conflict between Arab nations and Israel continued month by month, especially through forms of terrorism and reprisal attacks, though there were also major operations such as Israel's invasion of the Lebanon in 1982. Though greater moves towards peace were made in the 1990s, tension remained and military action made an appearance with depressing regularity.

The common hostility felt by many Arab nations towards Israel by no means prevented inter-Arab conflicts. The Gulf states in particular, with their exceptional reserves of internationally valuable oil, had an especially volatile relationship with one another after 1945. Between 1980 and 1988, Iran and Iraq were locked in a ferocious war over territorial rights to the Shatt-el-Arab waterway which separates the two countries. The resulting stalemate sucked huge resources out of both countries, and the disregard for human life on each side led to truly appalling death tolls.

The Gulf War

The next decade, the 1990s, began with another war in the Gulf states, this time as Iraq invaded and occupied its neighbour Kuwait after making a series of spurious claims to oil rights and related financial compensation. This time, however, the conflict was to escalate well beyond the bounds of the Middle East. An enormous coalition force of some 16 nations raised a huge military presence in Saudi Arabia and gave Saddam Hussein a deadline for withdrawal of his forces from Kuwait. The coalition army, which included a massive US and European presence, was a sign of how important this region was to international stability, and the world watched the clock with trepidation as the deadline approached. The deadline expired and the unfortunate Iraqi army received annihilating punishment in a prolonged and massive air assault and an armoured ground assault, which by 28 February 1991 had pushed Iraq back out of Kuwait. Despite the heavy western presence in the coalition, the largest numbers of ground troops were made up of those from other Middle Eastern states, particularly Saudi Arabia, Egypt and Syria, who felt threatened by Saddam Hussein's expansionism. Since the end of the formal conflict, a coalition presence has been maintained in the Middle East which even at the end of the decade pursued air attacks on Iraq in an attempt to make Iraq's weapons programme comply with UN resolutions.

The involvement of the West in the Gulf War was only part of the military investment made in the Middle East by outside countries after 1945. As in South East Asia and Africa, the Cold War brought Soviet and US interest into the region, and consequently the equipment and armaments of both these countries are very much apparent in Arab armies. Some, such as those of Egypt and Iran, displayed both sources of equipment, as sudden changes in political allegiance or religious affiliation made a rapid switch between suppliers necessary.

At the end of the 1990s, continuing tensions in the Middle East kept the Arab armies in a constant state of readiness. The soldiers of Middle Eastern armies varied greatly in quality and professionalism, yet some of them were amongst the most battle-experienced troops in the world. The fact that they will continue to be used in active service into the twenty-first century is, unfortunately for the prospects of peace in the region, almost a certainty, though perhaps the major conventional wars of the past are less likely, and more investment will go into fighting the ongoing presence of terrorism. Peace is making slow progress in several arenas, but it is clear that peace has a huge amount of history to overcome before the Middle East can become a place of stability.

▶ *Egyptian soldiers, lightly dressed in camouflage fatigues, practise their martial arts skills whilst preparing for the liberation of Kuwait in Desert Storm.*

Sergeant Arab Legion West Bank 1948

The Arab Legion was one of the most distinguished military units of the Middle East, with a combat record that stretched back to the 1920s under its British command. This command was to end in 1948 and Trans-jordan found itself fighting the newly created state of Israel over the possession of Jerusalem and the West Bank.

Despite the fact that Transjordan achieved political independence from Britain in 1946, British influence continued throughout the Arab Legion's organisation, equipment and uniforms. The sergeant here is preparing to fire a British 9mm Sten Mk V submachine gun, a model distinguished from earlier Stens by a pistol grip and a muzzle like the No.4 service rifle (this enabled fitting of a standard No.4 spike bayonet). The rest of his uniform is almost entirely of British manufacture: a standard khaki battle dress (including ankle gaiters) and 1937-pattern webbing, which here features two large ammunition pouches and a water bottle. Rank is conventionally denoted by three white chevrons on the sleeve, while the regimental colours of red/green/red are worn on the shoulder-strap slides and a lanyard around the left shoulder. The final piece of uniform, this time emphatically Arab, is the traditional shemagh head-dress, tied with a black agal and giving the silver Arab Legion badge prominence in the centre.

The Suez crisis in 1956 resulted in the Arab Legion's British connections becoming untenable, and from then on it was known as the Jordan Arab Army.

Date:	*1948*
Unit:	*Arab Legion*
Rank:	*Sergeant*
Location:	*West Bank*
Conflict:	*Arab-Israeli War*

Private Egyptian Army Southern Israel 1948

In 1948, on the very first day that Israel was established by the UN, the combined forces of much of the Arab world, including Egypt, Iraq, Syria and Transjordan, went on the attack against the fledging Jewish state. The Egyptian Army made its entry into the conflict by a bold invasion into Israel's southern territories.

The determined-looking infantryman here wears the standard uniform of the Egyptian Army for the late 1940s: a one-piece fly-fronted overall made from a khaki denim with one pocket on the left breast. This uniform was the same for either combat dress or fatigues. Khaki was the predominant cap colour for most units, as seen here, the exceptions being the cavalry, the military police and the artillery whose caps were green, red and black respectively. Cap badges were not worn by enlisted men in the Egyptian Army. Continuing British influences remain in the boots, garters and the Short Magazine Lee Enfield Mk III rifle with 1907-pattern bayonet. The webbing follows the British 1937 pattern and carries two large ammunition pouches at the front and a bayonet scabbard on the left hip.

The Egyptian invasion of Israel was a disaster, despite the heavy superiority on paper of the combined Arab forces over the incipient Israeli Defence Force (IDF). Outdated tactics and inadequate communication between combat groups resulted in heavy Egyptian casualties, and by 1949 Egypt was forced into an armistice without any gains.

Date:	*1948*
Unit:	*Egyptian Army*
Rank:	*Private*
Location:	*Southern Israel*
Conflict:	*Israeli Wars of Independence*

133

Private
Jordanian Army
West Jordan 1967

The Six-Day War was one of the Jordanian Army's most traumatic experiences. Though composed of vigorous and courageous fighters, Jordanian forces were practically obliterated under the immense assault of the Israel's tactically and logistically superior air and land attacks.

This soldier's uniform and equipment presents a typical Jordanian mix of British, US and local sources. The most definitively Jordanian feature is the fatigues themselves, which are made in a herring-bone twill khaki. The trousers are closed at the bottom with a pair of khaki anklets. The rest of the outfit is either British or US in origin. British features are the Mark 1 steel helmet with a camouflage netting cover and 1937-pattern webbing. The webbing belt here carries four ammunition pouches which would hold the eight-round clips taken by the US M1 rifle held by this soldier. Six million M1s were made between 1936 and 1959 and were distributed widely around the world, gaining favour with many soldiers for its reliable performance and stopping power.

The greatest territorial losses for Jordan during the Six-Day War were Jerusalem (of great significance in terms of its spiritual importance) and the West Bank of the Jordan. Yet the fighting on the Jordanian front cost the Israeli forces 1756 dead or wounded. These heavy casualties were incurred at the loss of over 6000 Jordanian troops and Israel was to formally acknowledge the tremendous bravery and tenacity of the Jordanian defence.

Date:	*1967*
Unit:	*Jordanian Army*
Rank:	*Private*
Location:	*West Jordan*
Conflict:	*Six-Day War*

Private Egyptian Commandos Sinai 1967

The year 1967 was a watershed for the Egyptian armed forces. Israel's brilliant execution of the Six-Day War, a pre-emptive strike on the Arab forces preparing to invade, meted out a severe defeat to the Egyptian troops occupying Sinai, and spotlighted Egypt's significant lack of tactical sophistication and quality weaponry – particularly her need for adequate air defences.

As was the case with many Middle Eastern armies during the Cold War, Soviet uniforms and equipment were supplied in bulk, and formed the most significant element of the Egyptian Army's fighting resources. The Egyptian commando here wears two main items of Soviet derivation: his steel helmet and the gas mask pack worn on his left hip. The rest of his uniform is of local manufacture, apart from the water bottle and its M1941 cover which are of a US origin. The overall camouflage worn here is a simple desert pattern, a natural choice for operations in the barren landscape of Sinai. His weapon is actually an Egyptian-made 9mm Port Said submachine gun. Its identical appearance to the Swedish Carl Gustav 45 is not coincidental: the Port Said is a Carl Gustav copy made under licence in Egypt.

After the Six-Day War, the Egyptian Army turned its hard military lessons into a more effective standing army, a transformation which was ultimately aided by stepping out from under the Soviet umbrella and taking more of its own tactical initiatives, based particularly on its experience of Israeli strengths.

Date:	*1967*
Unit:	*Egyptian Army Commandos*
Rank:	*Private*
Location:	*Sinai*
Conflict:	*Six-Day War*

Private Egyptian Army Sinai 1967

The domination of Soviet-supplied equipment and uniforms in the Egyptian Army was to last until the late 1970s, when US purchases started to show themselves. The infantryman pictured here demonstrates several items of Soviet apparel, but other influences are present and indicate the inferior state of supply in the Egyptian forces leading up to and during the Six-Day War.

The most recognisable item of Soviet origin is the 7.62mm AKM rifle, here held to the side with a fitted bayonet. Equally distinctive is the Soviet steel helmet, standard issue to many forces outside of the Soviet Bloc. This soldier's other equipment is minimal: a simple leather belt on which is hung a water canteen and, slung over the right shoulder, a small haversack, again of Soviet origin. The basic uniform of the Egyptian Army in 1967 was a two-piece set of light-khaki fatigues, the colour being ideally suited to the desert operations demanded by the Middle Eastern landscape. Soviet style as well as equipment seems evident here, as the soldier has a grey army blanket worn across his chest in the manner of the Soviet infantry seen on the Eastern Front during World War II. Wearing a blanket is far from incongruous in a theatre such as Sinai, for night temperatures drop extremely low in desert regions.

Departing from the Middle Eastern and Soviet sources are the soldier's web anklets, which are actually of the old British 1937 pattern, a remnant of British occupation in World War II.

Date:	*1967*
Unit:	*Egyptian Army*
Rank:	*Private*
Location:	*Sinai*
Conflict:	*Six-Day War*

Crewman Egyptian Armoured Forces 1973

On 14 October 1973, nearly 2000 main battle tanks came together in the Sinai desert and began the greatest tank battle since World War II. The conflict was the Yom Kippur War between Israel, Egypt and Syria and the tank battle was the Egyptian forces' last attempt to save an initially successful campaign against Israel's captured territories in Sinai and the Golan Heights.

When a massed attack of Syrian armour was defeated by the Israelis in the Golan Heights, it was left to the ranks of Egyptian T54/55 tanks to defeat the Israeli Centurions and M47/48 Pattons in the open spaces of Sinai. The Egyptian tank crewman pictured here shows the type of uniform that would have been worn in the Soviet MBTs. The 1955-issue sand-coloured shirt and trousers are worn with a padded canvas helmet that would have provided head-protection inside the cramped tanks, though the white fur lining, signifying a winter-issue, would have done little for comfort in the hot interior. The helmet would contain an internal headset, and also shown here is a throat microphone harness and, hanging down from the left shoulder, the lead for RT/IC internal communication radio.

The statistics of tank losses from 14 October reveal the scale of the Egyptian defeat: Egypt lost over 250 tanks for Israel's 10 tanks destroyed. After the early successes of the Yom Kippur conflict, this final blow for the Egyptian armoured troops must have been very bitter indeed.

Date:	*1973*
Unit:	*Egyptian Armoured Forces*
Rank:	*Crewman*
Location:	*West Sinai*
Conflict:	*Yom Kippur War*

137

Private
Syrian Army
Golan Heights 1973

By 1973, a series of military reforms had injected a much-needed professionalism into what was a demoralised and largely in-effective Syrian Army. This new sense of prestige was combined with extensive re-armament from Soviet sources. In 1973 a massed Syrian attack on the Israeli-controlled Golan Heights took the Israeli defenders largely by surprise.

The uniform, weapon and helmet of this Syrian soldier all speak of Soviet or Eastern Bloc sources. Held with its stock folded, the 7.62mm Kalashnikov AKMS rifle was the standard weapon of this time. This durable gun proved to be an excellent desert weapon as it was unlikely to jam, even under sandy conditions. Though the steel helmet is standard Soviet issue, the combat dress is not. East Germany is the most likely origin of the shirt and trousers, but the camouflage pattern is based on French patterning in the 1950s (such camouflage can commonly be seen on French paras in Indochina). Underneath his camouflaged shirt is an olive-drab Syrian Army shirt, and generally Syrian Army soldiers wore olive-drab or dark-khaki uniforms, which suggests that this soldier may belong to an elite regiment of some description. It is not unusual to see PLO soldiers in Syrian combat dress, as Syria was one of the PLO's major suppliers.

Despite a courageous assault by Syrian troops upon the Golan Heights, their tactical use of armour came unstuck in the mountainous terrain, and they once again experienced a heavy defeat.

Date:	*1973*
Unit:	*Syrian Army*
Rank:	*Private*
Location:	*Golan Heights*
Conflict:	*Syrian / Israeli War*

Guerrilla
Dhofari Guerrilla
Forces 1973

Dhofar is a province of Oman situated between harsh desert and the Arabian Sea and containing mountainous areas known as the jebel. Minor armed resistance to the Sultan of Oman's oppressive regime began in 1962, but by 1965 outside communist interests had taken over the jebel guerrillas' nationalistic cause and started a more aggressive campaign against the Sultan's Armed Forces (SAF).

The guerrillas' strength reached its peak – about 2000 men – in 1974. They became a notably effective force against the SAF, particularly through their use of a respectable arsenal of Soviet weaponry (including mortars, rocket launchers and even anti-aircraft missiles) supplied to them by the People's Democratic Republic of Yemen (PDRY). One example of this Soviet weaponry is carried by the guerrilla pictured here: the ubiquitous 7.62mm AKM assault rifle. The camouflage jacket is Soviet bloc, probably from East Germany, and is given in a leaf pattern typical of German experimentations in camouflage from World War II onwards. The exception to the communist influences is the British 1958-pattern web belt, though fitted with an AKM ammunition pouch. The headress and skirt are local traditional dress.

The guerrillas of Dhofar, by 1974 known as the Popular Front for the Liberation of Oman (or as the 'Adoo' by the SAF), were finally subjugated in that year by a mix of internal disagreements, more effective SAF actions and more judicious social policies from the Omani leadership.

Date:	*1973*
Unit:	*Dhofari Guerrilla Forces*
Rank:	*Guerrilla*
Location:	*Dhofar*
Conflict:	*Omani Civil War*

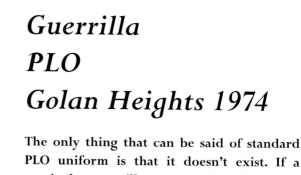

Guerrilla
PLO
Golan Heights 1974

The only thing that can be said of standard PLO uniform is that it doesn't exist. If a particular guerrilla was not dressed entirely in civilian clothes, then the 'uniform' would often include elements from places as diverse as the Soviet Union, East Germany, China, Syria, Jordan and a host of other Middle Eastern countries.

Despite this, the PLO could give the appearance of being a regular army, and even here there are certain identifiable stylistic features. The first, and most visible, is the famous shemagh head scarf, but the leather bomber jacket was also a popular form of clothing amongst operational PLO guerrillas (Syrian military jackets were also typical). The same applies to the jeans, T-shirt and sweatshirt which provided some kind of common look to members even when they were in civilian clothes. If webbing was worn, canvas chest webbing tended to be preferred. Much clothing and equipment was manufactured locally by the PLO.

The main weapon which this guerrilla carries is the Soviet 7.62mm Degtyarev RPD light machine gun, here fitted with a drum magazine, though he also carries an automatic pistol on his hip, the holster having an integral magazine holder.

Date:	*1974*
Unit:	*Palestinian Liberation Organisation*
Rank:	*Guerrilla*
Location:	*Golan Heights*
Conflict:	*Arab / Israeli Confrontation*

Private Iranian Revolutionary Guard Corps 1980

The Iranian Revolutionary Guard Corps (IRGC), or Pasdarin, suffered extraordinary losses during Iran's bloody eight-year war with Iraq. As the most numerous and ideologically motivated of Iran's forces, the IRGC led ill-conceived offensives which cost them hundreds of thousands of killed and wounded troops.

Pasdarin might demonstrate their commitment to Iranian revolutionary ideals by wearing red scarves around their necks. Yet the uniform of the IRGC often incorporated or repeated some features of the old pre-revolutionary Iranian Army, particularly the standard khaki fatigues and drill uniform. Another common form of dress was the two-piece olive-green fatigues pictured here, a uniform which, despite its prevalence, made no camouflage concessions to the desert regions in which the Gulf War fighting mainly took place. However, the economic and political insecurities of Iranian life often meant that dress could vary quite markedly between soldiers. The soldier here has a US M1 helmet but a British-type webbing which would usually hold fairly spartan supplies, such as a couple of ammunition pouches, a bayonet and a water bottle. The weapon in this case is the Heckler and Koch G3, but IRGC soldiers would just as likely be armed with FN-FAL, M16 or AK-series weapons. Up to the Revolution, when the Shah of Iran was overthrown, most weapons were acquired from the US, but the new regime switched its supplier to the Soviet Union.

Date:	*1980*
Unit:	*Iranian Revolutionary Guards Corps*
Rank:	*Private*
Location:	*Iran / Iraq Border*
Conflict:	*Gulf War*

Corporal
Iraqi Army
Shatt al Arab 1980

The Gulf War between Iran and Iraq lasted from 1980 until 1988 with huge costs on both sides in men and materials. While the equipment of Iraqi troops was mainly that of the Soviet Union and Western Europe, the uniforms could often lack consistency of appearance, and the quality of combat dress was generally low.

The two black stripes on this soldier's sleeve indicate the rank of corporal. Visible rank markings for NCOs of the Iraqi Army were quite limited, though officers would usually have their insignia in yellow or gold thread on an epaulette slide which matched their uniform colour. As this soldier would have been primarily operating in the desert border regions of Iran and Iraq, his uniform is an appropriate light khaki and the boots use lightweight 'desert' materials. Camouflage uniforms could also be found in different units of the Iraqi army (particularly the elite units) with patterns that reflected various other Middle Eastern and western colour schemes. Webbing equipment on Iraqi soldiers of this time – and into the next decade – tended to be kept to a minimum, often restricted to ammunition pouches, a water bottle and some simple provisions.

The soldier here follows this rule, the only visible pouches being the two for ammunition on his belt which would carry the magazines for his 7.62mm AKMS assault rifle. Completing this soldier's uniform is a black beret which bears the gold eagle emblem, an Iraqi national symbol.

Date:	*1980*
Unit:	*Iraqi Army*
Rank:	*Corporal*
Location:	*Shatt al Arab Waterway*
Conflict:	*Gulf War*

Private Lebanese Army Beirut 1982

From the late 1970s, the Lebanese Army was the beneficiary of US training and weaponry in its ongoing conflict against the various militia forces resident in its own country. This support, however, did not help them control Israel's invasion of the Lebanon in 1982 or solve the problems of religious factionalism that ran through the Army.

The Lebanese capital, Beirut, was a magnet for vicious street fighting in the 1980s, and the uniform of this Lebanese Army infantryman shows a complete focus on combat ability in an urban environment. His webbing and other equipment is purely firepower-related, consisting of nothing more than a 10-pouch ammunition belt. Each pouch carries a 20-round magazine for his 5.56mm M16A1 assault rifle, though the rifle itself is fitted with the curved 30-round magazine and a non-standard issue sling attached to the butt and foresight. The main uniform of the Lebanese Army was the ubiquitous olive-green fatigues finished with a pair of standard black leather boots. In this case, the soldier's headgear is a soft peaked cap, though in active combat conditions a steel helmet would be more usual for obvious reasons of general safety.

The Israeli invasion of the Lebanon precipitated the almost complete collapse of the Lebanese Army, and from 1983 until 1984 the Army found itself split by defeat at the hands of the Druze and Shi'ite Amal militias, after which factional allegiances further broke down any remaining military unity.

Date:	*1982*
Unit:	*Lebanese Army*
Rank:	*Private*
Location:	*Beirut*
Conflict:	*Lebanese Civil War*

Corporal Syrian Army Beirut 1982

The battle for Beirut in the early 1980s was a brutal product of Israel's military assaults on the Lebanon. Having decimated the Syrian forces in Operation Peace for Galilee, the IDF then tried to bomb the PLO out of existence in a 70-day siege which, in addition to the civilian population and the various guerrilla groups, trapped several thousand Syrian soldiers in the blighted city.

The soldier pictured here is probably a special forces soldier, a status indicated by the commando beret he is wearing. In this case, the uniform is the standard fatigues of Soviet pattern, such as was worn by most of the Syrian Army. However, Syrian commandos could also be seen in a distinctive 'lizard' pattern camouflage which featured a mix of khaki, browns and greens rendered in long brushstrokes. The chest webbing worn here continues the communist influence, being specifically designed to carry four of the 7.62mm AKM assault rifle's curving 30-round magazines.

The year 1982 was traumatic for the Syrian Army. Hundreds were killed in Operation Peace for Galilee and the airforce was absolutely decimated by Israeli fighters which gained complete air superiority. The subsequent siege of Beirut resulted in terrible suffering and on 21 August a multinational peace-keeping force evacuated some 3600 Syrian soldiers and over 10,000 Palestinian guerrillas and soldiers.

Date:	*1982*
Unit:	*Syrian Army*
Rank:	*Corporal*
Location:	*Beirut*
Conflict:	*Israeli Invasion of Lebanon*

Trooper Egyptian As-Saiqa Commandos 1980s

The special forces of Egypt are known as *As-Saiqa* (lightning) commandos. They have had to earn their title in actions ranging from fighting the Israeli forces along the Suez Canal from 1967 to 1970 to the Yom Kippur War in 1973 and counter-terrorist operations throughout the 1980s.

The Egyptian special forces were necessarily secretive about their modes of operation and their equipment, so details about uniforms can be sketchy. Hidden under a sand-coloured cover, the soldier pictured here shows few obvious indicators of standard uniform, especially as he is in extensive NBC (Nuclear, Biological, Chemical) gear. His boots and ankles are covered by anti-contamination covers and he is also wearing protective gloves and a respirator. In his right hand is a monitoring instrument for checking levels of chemicals or radiation. Egyptian commando camouflage is a distinctive brown-on-tan or green-on-tan patterning which provides good levels of visual disruption in a desert landscape. It is typically worn with black boots and, when on more ceremonial occasions, a black beret which bears the national badge, depicting an eagle. Personal weaponry varies, but this soldier is carrying a 7.62mm AK-74 assault rifle. The Belgian FAL assault rifle and Beretta M1951S are also popular.

Date:	*1980s*
Unit:	*As-Saiqa Commandos*
Rank:	*Trooper*
Location:	*Egyptian Desert*
Conflict:	*Unknown*

Africa

Africa's armies remain some of the world's most underdeveloped and unstructured military forces, though they are also amongst the most militarily active. The political and ethnic turbulence that dominates many African states has produced unpredictable armies and chaotic conflicts which tend to have a terrible impact upon civilians.

146

Africa

Few countries on earth have seen unbroken peace since the end of World War II, but as a continent Africa experienced more than its fair share of war. Many of its conflicts spun out of the vacuums left by departing colonial powers, vacuums which were filled by tribal rivalries, brutal political ambitions, territorial disputes and economic constraint, all catalysts for national violence. Some of Africa's wars were clear-cut battles between defined opponents, the government and UNITA guerrillas in Angola for instance, whereas others, such as in Sierra Leone, were incoherent bloodletting on the scale of war.

Yet perhaps the biggest thread tying all of Africa's wars together was the predominance of civil wars. Inter-country conflicts are certainly present in Africa's recent history, though even these often have internal ethnic implications, yet civil war blighted most of Africa's nations at some time or other and thus created a confusing picture of the armies within its vast boundaries.

The Colonial Shadow

Though there is no single origin behind Africa's turbulent history in the twentieth century, the presence and departure of its colonial powers must rank as its biggest single influence. At the end of World War II, much of Africa was under the colonial rule of various regimes, particularly those of the UK, France and Portugal. Yet from 1945 onwards, colonial outposts worldwide started to fall as European powers found them either difficult and expensive to control or politically inexpedient in a changing cultural climate.

In Africa, some moves towards independence were peaceable, yet others produced cruel guerrilla wars which saw western armies deployed on a large scale to combat growing insurgency. In most cases, such as France's Algeria (1954–62), Britain's Kenya (1952–60) and Portugal's Angola and Mozambique, independence was not achieved by the guerrillas' outright military victory, though the fighting was never totally one-sided, but by the constant pressure they applied to the colonial powers' economies and foreign policies.

With independence came a whole new set of problems. In many cases, the forces that had been fighting the colonists turned on one another almost the second that independence was achieved. In Angola, for instance, the Portuguese colonists were faced by the MPLA, FNLA and UNITA guerrillas, yet once independence was obtained the new MPLA government found itself in a bloody civil war with the anti-communist FNLA.

One of the most painful legacies of civil wars is that enmities are often etched deeper into a country's collective psyche. Many of Africa's conflicts since World War II have rolled on an almost indefinite basis, accentuating tribal and social rivalries and increasing the number of atrocities with every new mutation. Thus as late as 1999, FNLA guerrillas and the Angolan Government were repeating a full-scale civil war. Eritrea secured independence from Ethiopia in 1993, yet the border dispute which continued between the two countries saw bombing operations conducted against each other also in 1999. And in the mid-1990s the perpetual hostility between Hutu and Tutsi tribes in Rwanda boiled over into a concentrated period of slaughter that cost the lives of nearly one million civilians.

Countries outside of Africa became increasingly reluctant to enter into such conflicts even as arbiters, for the unpredictable nature of African wars meant that the security of either aid workers or peacekeeping soldiers was very difficult to maintain. Peacekeeping operations in Somalia, for instance, resulted in the deaths of US and Pakistani UN troops in the hot and violent streets of Mogadishu, since which time the western powers tended to keep their contributions on a specifically economic or political level. It is tremendously difficult for an outside party to handle conflicts which shift like the sea in force and complexion, and western military analysts started to use phrases such as 'vandalism on the scale of war' to describe the tremendous breakdown in social order and tactical purpose in war zones like Sierra Leone. The complexity of African conflicts became such that they changed the direction of military thinking and the technology appropriate to more anarchic styles of warfare.

All African states have their own standing armies for national security, and if we were to define a general trend, it would be that in the latter part of the twentieth century, they became increasingly well armed yet without an accompanying increase of training or organisation. There are, of course many exceptions to all elements of this generalisation. White southern African armies, such as those of Rhodesia and South Africa itself, tended to be the best equipped and trained, if for no other reasons than their wealth and the military culture and training inherited from their European ancestry. Yet other African armies, like the Nigerian Federal Army, had reasonably organised and well-armed soldiers, though standards varied dramatically between individuals. Equally, there were a great many armies which were inadequately armed and existed in almost perpetual disorganisation. The problem for many African armies was the factionalism within ranks who were mostly involved in wars within their own country of origin. This was coupled with a frequently chronic lack of money, and underpaid soldiers are a great danger to any government. In 1998 the government of Zimbabwe had to send 35,000 troops on enforced leave because of lack of government funds.

Equipment Diversity

All these insecurities and variables added up to almost infinitely variable modes of equipment and dress between and within African armies. Sudan, for instance, in its time received military supplies from the UK, US, Soviet Union, China, Libya and Egypt, and this was reflected in the incredible diversity of aged military stock that made up the armoury. In clothes as well as weapons, African soldiers were often seen in a hybrid of international combat dress which strayed from the military into the civilian. Yet despite the frequently sketchy nature of investment in uniforms, Africa contributed some especially vivid forms of camouflage which made quite faithful imitations of surrounding natural patterns. Thus Zaire's soldiers wore leopard-skin pattern camouflage, and the Ivory Coast a black twig pattern. Gabon mixed purples, blacks and greys on a white background.

Often being poorly led and with confused motivations, African armies, as generally shifting entities, soon defied the categories in which they were placed. Some units achieved an elite status – units like the Rhodesian African Rifles and the distinguished Selous Scouts – but most armies received little formal or even informal training, though ironically their chances of seeing combat were notably higher than most other world armies.

There is no predicting the potential flashpoints of the future. A recent worrying development was the growing conflict between Angola, Congo, Zimbabwe, Namibia and Chad on the one side and Rwanda and Uganda on the other. The conflict arose over Rwanda and Uganda's support of a Tutsi rebellion against Angola's government and it raised the real possibility

◀ *Selous Scouts soldiers cross a stream deep in the Rhodesian bush. This enigmatic elite unit took survival and combat skills to astounding levels and inflicted a heavy toll on their enemy.*

▶ *A patrol from the South African Reconnaissance Rifles, dressed in lightweight uniforms and bush hats, checks a dugout for terrorist weapons or personnel.*

of a full-scale war across mid-Africa. The Tutsi and Hutu enmity remained as threatening as ever both for internal and inter-African affairs, yet there were many other conflicts simmering across the continent at the end of the twentieth century which were just as unpredictable and just as difficult to control.

For Africa, the multitude of wars that swept its length after 1945 have brought untold suffering to millions of civilians. Battling against a frequently unforgiving climate and a true poverty, the people of this great continent saw an appalling scale of murder and cruelty that we would find difficult to imagine. In the 1990s, there were signs that more African governments seemed to be moving towards political harmony, thus fuelling the hope that soldiers would become an increasingly less common sight across the continent.

Guerrilla Algerian National Liberation Army 1960

The *Armée de Libéracion Nationale* (**ALN**) grew out of scattered nationalist forces which had started fighting the French colonists in November 1954. Established in 1956, the ALN set up a formal structure and chain of command, but it was to suffer terribly under French military supremacy and lost large numbers of men before independence was finally granted.

In 1959, the ALN received more and more Soviet weaponry and equipment through Egyptian channels, but the ALN had to arm and dress itself to a large extent on what could be taken from the French. The US equipment and dress present with the soldier here is explained by France's own dependence on US military provisions following World War II. His jacket is of the US M1943 variety and his matching olive-drab trousers are from the French forces. His headgear is a common peaked field cap adopted by many ALN soldiers in preference to helmets, while his footwear, a pair of ankle-length suede boots, are of civilian origin but ideal for the burning Algerian climate. Slung across his back is another mainstay of the US forces: the .30in M2 carbine. Unlike the earlier M1, the M2 had a full automatic capability though its effective range was very short, about 183m (200yds). On the whole, this soldier is well-equipped for an ALN combatant, a fact which implies that he is based across the border from Algeria in Tunisia, as the Algerian-based troops tended to lack adequate resources.

Date:	*1960*
Unit:	*Algerian National Liberation Army*
Rank:	*Guerrilla*
Location:	*Tunisian / Algerian Border*
Conflict:	*Algerian Independence War*

Mercenary
5 Commando
Katanga 1964

Mercenaries are by their very nature parasitic upon times of civil unrest, and the brutal string of conflicts that plagued the Congo (Zaire) for much of the 1960s was to provide diverse employment for many mercenaries from around the world.

This mercenary is clearly identified on his sleeve as a member of 5 Commando, one of the more unified and focused mercenary groups operating in the Congo. His green beret is the distinguishing mark of a commando, while the beret badge is of a Belgian armoured battalion (Belgian force badges were typical of 5 Commando insignia and mercenaries in general in the Congo, as the latter was until independence a Belgian colony). Belgian influences are continued in the smock and bayonet fitting for the redoubtable 7.62mm FN-FAL rifle, though the smock is recognisably based on the British paratroopers' Denison smock with its subtle green, brown and olive camouflage. Likewise, the Belgian webbing is also based on a British model, in this case a 1937-pattern belt with a holster for an automatic pistol such as a Colt .45 or a Browning 9mm.

The mercenaries of the Congo varied tremendously in both their motives and discipline and it was ultimately their lack of coherence that emasculated them as a force capable of changing the political future of the Congo. In 1967 there were some major mercenary operations, but these resulted in nothing other than retreat and signalled the end of real mercenary influence in the Congolese conflict.

Date:	*1964*
Unit:	*5 Commando*
Rank:	*Mercenary*
Location:	*Katanga Province*
Conflict:	*Congolese Civil War*

Major
5 Commando
Leopoldville 1964

Mercenaries were involved in the conflict in the Congo from 1960, but in 1964 Major Mike Hoare introduced a new level of professionalism and discipline into the mercenary world. His unit of troops, known as 5 Commando, achieved exceptional results over the Simba rebels through their financially motivated support for the regime of Moise Tshombe.

The appearance of Major Hoare in the illustration here is very much that of a British officer in tropical uniform, with a commando beret suggesting the perceived prestige of his military force. The short-sleeved service shirt bears the 5 Commando name badge while the rank of Major is indicated on the shoulder slides. Typically for mercenaries in the Congo at this time, the rank insignia generally follows the form of the Belgian Army, the insignia of Major being a single yellow bar and star: the dagger motif is a commando addition. His combat trousers are neatly tucked into a pair of British-issue anklets. The web belt is a British 1944 pattern, on which he carries a small compass pouch and, on his right hip, a revolver.

Mike Hoare sought to create a military unit that was as controlled and ordered as any regular army unit. The 5 Commando were undoubtedly effective, and managed to operate as a cohesive unit in contrast to many of the other mercenary units attracted to the region. In 1965 Major Mike Hoare became Lieutenant Colonel Mike Hoare for his military achievements in the Congo.

Date:	*1964*
Unit:	*5 Commando*
Rank:	*Major*
Location:	*Leopoldville*
Conflict:	*Congolese Civil War*

Private Biafran Army East Nigeria 1968

The torn and inconsistent appearance of this soldier illustrates the constant lack of materials and equipment which plagued the Biafran Army in their three-year campaign for independence from Nigeria.

This soldier's generally military appearance would often have been the only thing to identify him with his comrades. Headgear alone ranged from the khaki jungle hat worn here through to Soviet and US helmets with camouflaged covers. Likewise, clothing would have moved across all manner of items that had a look of combat dress. Here the soldier wears a khaki shirt and olive-green trousers with a pair of very civilian wellington boots. The only item this man has on his web belt is an ammunition pouch for the magazines of his 7.62mm Vz58 assault rifle, a Czech copy of the Soviet AK-47. Numbering some 40,000 men at its peak strength, the Biafran Army had no external suppliers of military equipment, unlike its well-armed and numerically superior opponents, the Nigerian Army. Consequently, the Biafran soldiers had to kit themselves out in what was either locally to hand or, particularly in the case of arms, what could be captured from the enemy.

Despite this handicap and their eventual defeat in 1970, the Biafran Army was an enthusiastic and persistent body of fighters who kept the formal strength of Nigeria at bay for much longer than expected. In the end, it was more a case of strategic mistakes than a lack of combat effectiveness that led to their final defeat.

Date:	*1968*
Unit:	*Biafran Army*
Rank:	*Private*
Location:	*East Nigeria*
Conflict:	*Biafran War*

Private Nigerian Federal Army 1968

Nigeria's civil war (1967–70) was to show up the severe faultlines running through the Nigerian Federal Army's (NFA) structure and tactics. Though the Federal Army did have some professional officers, a series of political coups and defections to the Biafran cause left the army with too few individuals capable of handling a rapidly expanding military organisation, and their eventual victory can be accredited to sheer scale of numbers and equipment rather than expertise.

Unlike many African armies, the Nigerian Federal Army was able to kit out many of its soldiers with high-quality weapons and outfits, though supply lines did become stretched as the army expanded. This soldier wears the instantly recognisable US M1 helmet and his fatigues are standard NFA combat dress, though NFA soldiers of this time can also be seen in khaki outfits. Perhaps the most interesting item of clothing here is the footwear: a pair of British Army jungle boots purpose-made out of canvas and rubber. The boots are not alone in being of British origin. Gripped in his hands is the 9mm Mk II Sten submachine gun, the ammunition for which he keeps in the two large ammunition pouches at his waist. These pouches and the webbing belt are British 1958 pattern, while the water bottle on his right hip is 1944 pattern. Other weapons commonly seen with the NFA are the FN-FAL rifle and the G3 rifle. The many British elements are indicative of Nigeria's colonial past, as Nigeria only achieved independence in 1960.

Date:	*1968*
Unit:	*Nigerian Federal Army*
Rank:	*Private*
Location:	*Biafra*
Conflict:	*Biafran War*

Crewman Chadian National Army 1970

The civil wars which followed Chad's independence in August 1960 saw the Chadian Army fall under a varied succession of leadership, title and government. France's involvement as a former colonist in Chad's politics and commerce provided one of the few strands of continuity for the Chadian Army in terms of its weapons and training.

The Panhard AML-60 and AML-90 were the main French armoured cars commonly employed by the Chadian Army, and this man here is a crew member of one such vehicle. The French theme continues with the soldier's armoured fighting vehicle (AFV) communication headphones and the generally French components of his uniform, including his boots and his paratrooper's shirt. The exception to this European dress is the bayonet for the Chinese Type 56 assault rifle hanging from the elasticated cord around his waist. As with any army whose history and finances have been turbulent, the Chadian Army equipped itself from a multitude of sources, and American and Soviet Bloc materiels have all made their impression on the appearance of Chad's national force.

In 1970 the civil war was broadly divided along the lines of north against south, though this picture became dramatically more complex in 1975 following the execution of the Chadian leader, François Tombalbaye, during a military coup. Factionalism consequently sank its fingers deeper into Chad's Army and since 1975, its status as a unified military force became somewhat academic.

Date:	1970
Unit:	Chadian National Army
Rank:	Crewman
Location:	Central Chad
Conflict:	Chadian Civil War

Mercenary FNLA Angola 1975

Angola's independence wars against Portuguese colonial rule found significant numbers of mercenaries being recruited into the anti-Portuguese causes. The *Frente Nacional de Libertação de Angola* (FNLA) in particular attracted many mercenary soldiers from a variety of Western and African nations.

By virtue of their non-orthodox status, mercenaries tended to dress in whatever was at hand. In Angola that usually meant Soviet or US army surplus or captured Portuguese equipment. This white FNLA mercenary is dressed with great simplicity. His olive drab uniform is matched by a peaked bush hat with a neckpiece at the back (useful sun protection under the Angolan skies). The only equipment he carries is his firearm, the ever-present Soviet 7.62mm AKM. Due in the main to the heavy Soviet involvement in the affairs of the African continent during the Cold War, the AKM was – even into the 1990s – one of the most common military firearms in African conflicts. Some 11,000 Portuguese troops were killed within the three territories of Angola, Mozambique and Portuguese Guinea by 1975. In Angola, the FNLA's objectives were severely weakened by a lack of political and military strategy. When independence did finally come to Angola in 1975, it was the Marxist MPLA which took power, despite the fact that the FNLA had been supported in its cause by both the USA and South Africa. In the ensuing civil war on the Portuguese departure, the FNLA were beaten comprehensively by MPLA forces.

Date:	*1975*
Unit:	*FNLA*
Rank:	*Mercenary*
Location:	*Angola*
Conflict:	*Angolan Independence War*

Private Rhodesian African Rifles 1976

The Rhodesian African Rifles (RAR) was an effective and capable counter-insurgency force during the Rhodesian civil war of the 1970s. Formed in 1940, the RAR took its experience of anti-guerrilla warfare in 1950s Malaya and employed it in its operations against the ZANU and ZAPU nationalist units.

This RAR soldier's camouflaged uniform reflects the conditions of African operations with a mixture of brown, khaki and olive-green in a foliage-style pattern. The uniform material is cotton and the field cap displays the RAR badge on a green-and-black field. The webbing is of British 1958 pattern. Visible on this soldier's belt are two large water bottles, an ammunition pouch and two South African kidney pouches used to hold various essential equipment. The boots, probably South African made, are notable for their buckled cuff sections which derived from US patterns from World War II.

The weapon the soldier is carrying is a classic infantry support firearm that achieved popularity with many forces around the world: the 7.62mm FN machine gun. As the RAR's role in the Rhodesian conflict was generally that of counter-insurgency in the African bush, it has been camouflaged.

Date:	*1976*
Unit:	*Rhodesian African Rifles*
Rank:	*Private*
Location:	*Rhodesian Bush*
Conflict:	*Rhodesian Civil War*

157

Private
Selous Scouts
South Rhodesia 1977

Of all the combat units operating in Rhodesia's long-standing civil war, the Selous Scouts must go down as the most exceptional. Trained as an elite reconnaissance and counter-guerrilla unit, their fieldcraft, combat skills and toughness made them a legendary force, despite their brief six-year existence. They numbered only 1500 men at peak strength, yet according to a Combined Operations statement, they inflicted 68 per cent of the nationalist guerrilla fatalities between 1973 and 1980.

Compared to many pictures of operational Selous Scouts, the soldier here is almost overdressed. All Selous Scouts travelled light and without a formal uniform, often being seen dressed in nothing but shorts and training shoes (in this case hockey boots, or 'tackies'), while carrying only their weapon, ammunition and a water canteen. As their duties were mainly clandestine tracking, observation and assassination roles, all conducted within the heat of the Rhodesian sun, nothing inessential was carried and they often had to live off the land during operations.

The standard weapon of the Selous Scouts was the 7.62mm FN-FAL rifle, usually camouflaged. This soldier's shirt is in a typical Rhodesian foliage pattern. Webbing was a mixture of styles and origins, though the British 1958-pattern webbing was prevalent, which the soldier here wears with ammunition pouches, water bottle and a kidney bag.

Date:	*1977*
Unit:	*Selous Scouts*
Rank:	*Private*
Location:	*South Rhodesia*
Conflict:	*Rhodesian Civil War*

Guerrilla Eritrean Liberation Front 1979

The Ethiopean annexation of Eritrea in 1962 precipitated a long-running war between nationalist Eritrean guerrillas and the Ethiopean regular army. Resistance to Ethiopean rule from Eritrea was vigorous, and in 1993 Eritrea was finally recognised as an independent state by Ethiopia, though border disputes continued after that date.

The Eritrean Liberation Front (ELF) constituted an effective guerrilla force, despite its tendency towards infighting and fighting with other independence groups. In terms of its uniform, the most common form of dress was a two-piece khaki outfit worn with simple training shoes or sandals. However, as the ELF was a guerrilla force with all the accompanying supply problems and irregularities, this description should be treated with some caution. All types of civilian dress and military equipment would be pressed into service by the guerrillas, as the soldier opposite illustrates. His denim shirt, lightweight trousers, plimsolls and colourful headscarf are all of civilian origin. The only items which define his combat status are his British 1937-pattern webbing with ammunition pouch, and his firearm. Soviet or Soviet-bloc weapons were common amongst Eritrean guerrillas, supplied to them by sympathetic Arab nations. This soldier carries a Cz58, a Czech assault rifle which fired the same 7.62mm cartridge as the Soviet AK-47, and indeed bore quite a striking resemblance to that weapon, despite differences in its gas-operated mechanism.

Date:	*1979*
Unit:	*Eritrean Liberation Front*
Rank:	*Guerrilla*
Location:	*Eritrea*
Conflict:	*Eritrean Independence War*

Guerrilla Rhodesian Patriotic Front 1979

The Rhodesian Patriotic Front was born from the union of two nationalist organisations: the Zimbabwe African National Union (ZANU) and the Zimbabwe African People's Union (ZAPU). Its unrelenting, if disorganised, action against white Rhodesian rule was the major factor in the eventual creation of black-ruled Zimbabwe.

The uniform of the Patriotic Front guerrilla pictured here demonstrates the opportunism upon which all unconventional armies rely. The camouflage trousers and leather boots (with anklets) are items captured from his conventional Rhodesian Army opponents, and the camouflage pattern is ideal for blending into the Rhodesian bush. The uniform is completed with whatever is at hand, in this case a green T-shirt and green beret. The latter was by no means standard, and Patriotic Front headgear showed the usual range of styles from soft peaked caps and bush hats to steel helmets. The only webbing this man wears is four ammunition pouches strung across his chest which hold ammunition for his 7.62mm Heckler and Koch G3 rifle.

Wearing ammunition to the front of the body was typical of Patriotic Front dress, and if the soldier was armed with an AK assault rifle (as many Patriotic Front men were), then he would probably wear the curved 'ChiCom' (Chinese Communist) chest ammunition pouches, which were also favoured by the Selous Scouts for their accessibility and physical convenience in combat operations.

Date:	*1979*
Unit:	*Rhodesian Patriotic front*
Rank:	*Guerrilla fighter*
Location:	*Rhodesia / Zimbabwe*
Conflict:	*Rhodesian Civil War*

Private South African Army Namibia 1980

In 1966 the territory of South-West Africa was taken from South African control by the UN and renamed Namibia. South Africa repudiated the action, and increased its jurisdiction over the region despite increasing attacks by the South West African People's Organisation (SWAPO) guerrillas based in Angola.

As with all South Africa's soldiers, this particular infantryman's uniform is designed for comfort in high temperatures. The shirt and trousers are made of a lightweight material, the pockets of the trousers and jacket having hidden buttons to avoid their snagging on straps and foliage. Typically for 1980, the South African webbing would hold a water bottle positioned in the small of the soldier's back which was flanked by two kidney pouches, one of which would feature a bayonet attachment. Coming around the waist, and visible in this illustration, are two pairs of ammunition packs which would contain the magazines for the 7.62mm FN-FAL rifle. The webbing was also designed to carry a backpack over the whole kit if needed and there were fittings to hang a poncho roll directly beneath the water bottle and kidney pouches.

Throughout the 1980s, the South African Army was involved in supporting anti-government UNITA guerrilla forces in Angola and trying to keep Namibia out of Angolan control. However, a peace agreement in 1988 gave independence to Namibia and stopped South African involvement in internal Angolan affairs.

Date:	*1980*
Unit:	*South African Army*
Rank:	*Private*
Location:	*Namibia*
Conflict:	*Namibia*

Sergeant South African Recon Commando 1990s

In the 1990s, only about eight per cent of the people who embarked on the 42 weeks' training for the South African Reconnaissance Commando actually passed the course. Those that did pass became part of an elite force of counter-terrorist experts, with formidable capacities in tracking, survival and engagement in the African bush.

All Reconnaissance Commandos, or 'Recces' as they were informally known, would be fully trained in parachute techniques, including free fall and HALO (High Altitude Low Opening) jumps. Their uniform and equipment took account of this as the strong webbing held a double-sided rucksack with a space in the middle for a parachute to be added. The standard uniform in a sand-brown colour provided good cover in the African bush, though several commando-pattern camouflages were available which varied from a dark mix of blue, black and grey colours to lighter sand and khaki shades. This soldier also displays the simple floppy bush hat worn by most of South Africa's special forces.

On the soldier's webbing here are two ammunition pouches for the 5.56mm Galil rifle (South Africa being a major export market for this Israeli firearm), plus two rifle grenades, a smoke canister and a water bottle. In operational circumstances, white Recce soldiers were usually seen with completely blacked faces to disguise their identity at a distance when in areas inhabited by mainly black South Africans.

Date:	*1990s*
Unit:	*S. African Reconnaissance Commandos*
Rank:	*Sergeant*
Location:	*South African Bush*
Conflict:	*None*

Asia

The continent of Asia has suffered many wars large and small since the end of World War II, including the international struggles of the Cold War in Korea and Vietnam. Such wars have not only affected those living directly in the path of the warring armies, but have also altered the West's understanding of the limits of technology.

Modern Military Uniforms

A large part of history in post-World War II Asia was the steady expulsion of colonial influences from the region, especially in South-East Asia. World War II was a watershed in colonial history, for after 1945 many western nations found that their colonies were no longer prepared to accept the jurisdiction of foreign power. Much of South-East Asia was in European hands, particularly British and French rule (other significant colonists being Portugal and Spain). In 1945, states such as Sri Lanka, Malaysia and Singapore were in British control, while Cambodia, Laos and Indochina were in the hands of the French. Twenty-five years later all these were in the hands of the indigenous peoples, the colonists being expelled by a mix of guerrilla attacks, political pressure and outright war.

The impressive element of many of these conflicts is the duration for which they ran. The Malayan 'Emergency', for example, lasted from 1948 to 1960, despite the level of sophistication reached by the British forces in counter-insurgency techniques. But in terms of scale, there were few bigger post-war conflicts than that fought by the French in Indochina between 1945 and 1954. Vietnamese communist forces, known collectively as the Viet Minh, immediately began combative operations when the French colonists attempted to reassert their control of the country following the expulsion of the Japanese occupiers in 1945. The Viet Minh walked the strategic path of revolutionary warfare laid down by Mao Tse-Tung and, in a gradual progression from guerrilla operations to open warfare, they engineered a French defeat by 1954, the French dead amounting to some 21,000 soldiers.

The expulsion of the French from Indochina did not bring peace to this troubled region of Asia. The war left Vietnam divided at the 17th parallel into northern and southern regions and this division was to bring a greater and more expansive strife to Vietnam from the 1960s onwards. This was because although the French war had in part been a colonial war, it was also very much a conflict of the Cold War.

For most of second half of the twentieth century, the powers of communism and capitalism were jockeying for position across the globe, often under the sponsorship of the superpowers. East Asia in particular was a virulent arena for this struggle, partly due to the solid communist presence of China in the region, partly due to the vacuum left by departing colonial powers, and no doubt partly due to the persuasive character of the communist philosophy itself amongst fairly poor rural communities.

Communist expansion in East Asia was of acute concern to the powers in Western Europe, the United States and the South Pacific. Thus the invasion of South Korea by communist North Korea in 1950 quickly escalated into a prodigious war involving 16 UN nations and China, as well as the two Korean nations.

▶ *A South Korean soldier takes aim during peacetime manoeuvres with a US soldier, the former's helmet, uniform, backpack and weapon testifying to the influence of US sponsorship.*

◀ *Few individual units were feared by the Viet Cong and NVA as much as South Korea's Tiger Division, who almost always wore densely patterned camouflage uniforms.*

164

The three-year Korean War saw little in the way of territorial change in East Asia, yet the whole region would remain a turbulent zone of Cold War anxiety. In the early 1960s, communist insurgency escalated in South Vietnam, and as the US tried to bolster South Vietnam's defences, the conflict developed into a ten-year war which cost the lives of well over one million Vietnamese, US and other nations' soldiers. This was a war which not only saw the eventual defeat of the US superpower and South Vietnam by the communist North, but also spiralled out into neighbouring countries such as Cambodia, Laos and Thailand. The legacy of the Vietnam War, apart from the tragic human damage, was a prevailing instability in South-East Asia which would set in train an exceptionally bloody revolution in Cambodia under Pol Pot and further conflict between Vietnam, Cambodia and Thailand and Laos in the 1970s and 1980s.

Afghanistan

In 1979, the Soviet Union invaded Afghanistan in an effort to maintain a communist regime there. Like the US in Vietnam, the Soviet Union found itself locked into a lengthy guerrilla war, and an inexorably rising casualty count and a changing political climate drove their troops out of Afghanistan in 1988.

This conflict on Russia's southern rim was a reminder that Asia's military struggles had not been confined to the east alone. Since the break-up of the Soviet Union in the early 1990s, stability was noticeably absent from many of the former Soviet republics. Countries such as Chechnya, Georgia, Moldova and Azerbaijan all saw fighting either against Russian forces or between various ethnic groups attempting to seize power or their own territorial independence. These countries remained potential and actual military flashpoints in the 1990s, particularly as the combination of deteriorating economies and the remaining mass of Soviet military equipment made aggression the more likely.

Despite these tensions and conflicts, Asia as a whole reached a greater level of stability by the end of the twentieth century than it had for many years, though from experience this situation could change in an instant.

Trooper
UN Partisan Infantry
North Korea 1952

The United Nations Partisan Infantry (UNPI) are one of the least known forces of the Korean War. Mostly composed of North Koreans opposed to their own communist government, the UNPI numbered some 22,000 soldiers and made a significant draw on enemy resources and men actually behind the North Korean lines.

The UNPI started out in their operations without a great deal of external support, but once the US started to perceive the significance of the UNPI contribution, military aid was forthcoming. US assistance explains the nature of this partisan soldier's dress, which comprises various elements of US Army clothing. The uniform is the olive-green herringbone twill two-piece jungle fatigues such as were issued to certain sectors of the US military, particularly the Marine Corps, in 1942 and were a common form of dress in the Pacific campaigns of World War II. He wears this uniform with a matching peaked soft cap. Suspended from a US M1936 web belt is the classic 9mm Browning pistol in a holster, an example of the type of firearms that would be received from the US. His combat boots are also of US manufacture.

Operating from bases within North Korea, the UNPI claimed to have taken over 69,000 lives from the North Korean Army and destroyed over 2700 of their vehicles by the ceasefire in 1953, claims which correspond with US estimates of the UNPI effectiveness in hampering the communist war effort throughout the conflict.

Date:	*1952*
Unit:	*United Nations Partisan Infantry*
Rank:	*Trooper*
Location:	*North Korea*
Conflict:	*Korean War*

Guerrilla Malayan Races Liberation Army 1953

The Malayan Races Liberation Army (MRLA) were aided in their struggle for Malaysian independence against the British by the weapons and experience their men had gained when fighting the Japanese during World War II. Despite the fact that they were heavily disadvantaged both politically and militarily, they maintained a determined campaign against the British for 12 years.

The MRLA was, to all intents and purposes, a guerrilla army, yet it still managed to give a common military look to its soldiers through both its own locally produced clothing and Japanese war surplus. The soldier pictured opposite wears a typical khaki drill shirt and trousers, the latter being bound up to the knee in matching puttees in a style reminiscent of that of the Japanese Army. His communist allegiance is given testimony through the red star on his five-pointed peaked khaki cap. A departure for military orthodoxy is in his footwear – rubber and canvas basketball boots – though such light and flexible footwear was popular with Far Eastern guerrillas of all nations throughout the latter half of the twentieth century. British influences are introduced in the 1937-pattern webbing and the Short Magazine Lee Enfield (SMLE) Rifle No.1 Mk III. The ammunition for his rifle is worn in a five-pouch canvas bandolier worn around the waist. One actual piece of Japanese war surplus is the water bottle, part of the large amount of Japanese stock held over from the occupation.

Date:	*1953*
Unit:	*Malayan Races Liberation Army*
Rank:	*Guerrilla*
Location:	*Rural Malaya*
Conflict:	*Malayan 'Emergency'*

Guerrilla Viet Minh Dien Bien Phu 1954

The Viet Minh of the Indochina War were separated into three different types: a village militia; regional troops; and the Chuc Luc, the regular army. These types formed an escalating scale of professionalism and combat readiness, but combined, they were a truly formidable opponent which the French Army ultimately found too strong to resist.

The black 'pyjamas' uniform worn by the soldier here marks him out as one of the Chuc Luc, a force of some 125,000 troops (1954) which fought as a conventional army in every aspect of strategy, weaponry and structure. Though a variety of fatigue and combat dress could be seen in the Chuc Luc, especially olive-green fatigues of Chinese origin, the black outfit here acted almost as a standard uniform, whereas the regional troops and village militia tended to dress entirely as civilians to support their more guerrilla-style activities. Chinese support influenced both weaponry and clothing, and indeed Chinese troops were in direct action against the French at Dien Bien Phu.

This soldier is wearing a French Army tropical hat, but the most common form of Viet Minh headwear was the classic Vietnamese cork helmet, designed to protect the head whilst allowing air to circulate. French equipment also plays an important part in this soldier's combat ability, as he is armed with the 9mm MAT 49 submachine gun, a portable and compact weapon that was popular with French paratroopers and infantry.

Date:	*1954*
Unit:	*Viet Minh*
Rank:	*Guerrilla*
Location:	*Dien Bien Phu*
Conflict:	*Indochina War*

Private North Vietnamese Army 1954

The year 1954 signalled the NVA's monumental victory over French forces at Dien Bien Phu. Situated in north-west Tongking, Dien Bien Phu was intended to be an outpost for French anti-guerrilla operations and also to draw Viet Minh forces into open battle. Yet Vietnamese forces imposed a 55-day siege from the surrounding hills with constant attacks and artillery bombardments, all the while stopping French resupply through heavy anti-aircraft fire. The French surrender was inevitable and pushed France into their final withdrawal from Indochina.

The soldier pictured here reflects the North Vietnamese celebrations of 1954. His dress is absolutely typical of the NVA (including the NVA during the later war with South Vietnam and the US). The olive-green uniform is a simple two-piece shirt and trousers, the latter having button fastenings at the ankle for practicality in jungle conditions. Footwear is a pair of canvas plimsolls and the webbing consists here of a simple belt on which hangs a machete and a water-bottle cover acting as an ammunition pouch. The hat is made from woven reeds with a cloth cover, though the NVA could also be seen in colonial-style pith helmets or peaked field caps.

Colonial influence is more directly apparent here in the soldier's firearm: the 7.5mm French MAS 1936 rifle was the standard weapon of French forces throughout the 1950s, and this soldier's weapon has probably been captured from them.

Date:	*1954*
Unit:	*North Vietnamese Army*
Rank:	*Private*
Location:	*Hanoi*
Conflict:	*Indochina War*

Guerrilla Viet Cong South Vietnam 1966

The Viet Cong was one of the most competent guerrilla armies in twentieth-century history, and maintained a steadily increasing casualty count for US, ARVN and allied forces patrolling in South Vietnam.

The defining Viet Cong uniform was the classic black pyjama outfit consisting of a loose, collarless jacket with matching trousers that varied between ankle and calf length. Footwear was equally distinctive – rubber sandals cut directly from old motor tyres – an economical improvisation typical of Viet Cong practicality and austerity. Webbing would often be a single belt of either Eastern Bloc or Vietnamese origin supported by web or cloth shoulder braces, with equipment and rations carried in pouches from captured enemies or local manufacture.

An active Viet Cong irregular would survive in the field on an almost exclusive diet of rice, and the soldier pictured here shows the usual method of transporting this food: in a roll wrapped around the body. This soldier's headgear is a standard khaki pith helmet which would most likely be covered by camouflaged net or material when in combat conditions, though the Viet Cong also wore the usual variety of cloth bush hats and, generally when not fighting, the traditional conical palmleaf hat of the Asian peasantry.

The soldier pictured here carries a piece of Soviet weaponry, the RPG-2, a shoulder-fired grenade launcher with a round capable of punching through 330mm (13in) of armour at up to 500m (1640ft).

Date:	*1966*
Unit:	*Viet Cong*
Rank:	*Guerrilla*
Location:	*South Vietnam*
Conflict:	*Vietnam War*

Guerrilla Viet Cong South Vietnam 1967

During the Vietnam War, the Viet Cong demonstrated incredible industry, nerve and tactical awareness through their construction of an extensive defensive tunnel system in South Vietnam. The tunnels were prodigious in scale, often stretching for hundreds of metres with multiple levels and entry points, and they proved an unwelcome and nerve-wracking obstacle for US troops to overcome.

The entries to the tunnels were often incredibly small to prevent easy access by US soldiers, who tended to be of greater physical size than the shorter and less well-fed Viet Cong. Pictured here is one of the tunnel fighters, the absence of helmet being a practical omission for unhindered movement down the claustrophobic passages. He is dressed in typical items of Viet Cong clothing: black 'pyjama' trousers, a khaki combat shirt and three-pouch chest webbing to carry magazines for his 7.62mm AK-47 assault rifle. The footwear is the classic rubber sandals, cut directly from vehicle tyres.

Soldiers such as this one used the tunnels for three main purposes. Firstly, sitting deep within the laterite soil provided superb protection from the heavy US air strikes. Secondly, the tunnels were perfect for storing arms and equipment close to the combat zone or US targets without being discovered. Thirdly, the Viet Cong could conduct surprise attacks on the enemy forces before vanishing back into the labyrinthine passages. When tunnels were discovered by US forces, the process of clearing them often proved costly.

Date:	*1967*
Unit:	*Viet Cong*
Rank:	*Guerrilla fighter*
Location:	*South Vietnam*
Conflict:	*Vietnam War*

Private
RoK Capital Division
Vietnam 1969

Part of the Republic of Korea's (RoK) contribution to the Vietnam War was the ROK Capital Division. This capable fighting unit soon created fear in the Viet Cong ranks on account of its cruel but effective fighting methods, methods very much symbolised by the 'Tiger' label derived from the Capital Division's badge.

The Tiger badge was literally just that: an image of the head of a roaring tiger placed on a green shield background and worn as a shoulder patch. Naturally the history of South Korea meant that US equipment was very prevalent amongst the Korean troops in Vietnam, and here we see a Capital private dressed in several items or versions of US dress. The robust camouflage pattern is actually an ROK adaptation of the camouflage outfits used by US during the Pacific campaigns of World War II and over this he is wearing a US M1955 flak vest. The helmet is also of US origin – the common M1 – and this has a camouflage cover to match the uniform itself. His weapon is the standard issue US 5.56mm M16A1.

Korean forces fought well in Vietnam, though there was a political awkwardness about operating under US auspices, so US strategies for operations were communicated through 'requests' rather than commands. Even so, by 1969 the Capital Division had killed around 12,400 enemy soldiers, and when they left Vietnam in 1973 they did so with a particularly strong fighting reputation.

Date:	*1969*
Unit:	*RoK Capital Division*
Rank:	*Private*
Location:	*South Vietnam*
Conflict:	*Vietnam War*

First Lieutenant ARVN Vietnam 1970

By 1970, the Army of the Republic of South Vietnam (ARVN) was starting to feel its isolation as the US forces began a steady withdrawal from the war. Yet in an attempt to give the ARVN more of a fighting capability against the Viet Cong and North Vietnamese troops, from 1968 the US gave heavy material support, with the result that most ARVN soldiers are dressed in a US manner.

Though the 'Tigerstripe' pattern of camouflage was a trademark pattern of US Special Forces, the actual print was a product of the Vietnamese Marine Corps dating back to 1959. Many Vietnamese soldiers continued to wear this pattern even under the influx of other US patterns of camouflage. This soldier is wearing Tigerstripe combat dress and a jungle hat which features his rank: two gold blossoms indicating the rank of First Lieutenant in the South Vietnamese Army. A distinctive piece of non-US dress is the nylon mesh waistcoat with integral pockets for ammunition and supplies. The web belt is the US M1967 pattern and hung on the belt are two M26A2 fragmentation grenades and an automatic pistol in a holster.

The soldier's main weapon is the 5.56mm M16A1 rifle, the standard US rifle used in the war. The M16 was of a small calibre, yet its muzzle velocity was so high that even a hit on a non-vital area of the body could kill the victim through trauma alone, such was the effect of its impact.

Date:	*1970*
Unit:	*ARVN*
Rank:	*First Lieutenant*
Location:	*South Vietnam*
Conflict:	*Vietnam War*

Guerrilla Khmer Rouge Cambodia 1975

The violent excesses of the Khmer Rouge, especially under the leadership of the mentally precarious leader Pol Pot, have been well documented. By 1975, the Khmer Rouge had established political authority over Kampuchea after a protracted civil war against the army of Prince Sihanouk, and started to enforce a reign of terror against the civilian population, an estimated one million people being slaughtered through ideological genocide.

The Khmer Rouge had, for a time at least, extensive supply lines through North Vietnam and China, so it is common to see their soldiers dressed in the olive-green or dark-brown uniforms of those nations. The cap worn here, for example, appears to be the same type as that worn by the Chinese Liberation Army. Yet in general, the soldier here shows a much more typical image of the Khmer Rouge, clad in the classic black clothing of the peasant population and using the cheap yet functional open sandals as footwear. Colourful headscarves were also common, with red-and-white colour schemes being particularly prevalent, though this soldier wears a blue-and-white variation around his neck.

The ammunition pouches carried on the guerrilla's webbing are of the 'ChiCom' (Chinese Communist) variety, being purpose-designed to carry the curved magazines for the 7.62mm Type 56 assault rifle, the Chinese version of the AK47. They were very popular for their easy accessibility.

Date:	*1975*
Unit:	*Khmer Rouge*
Rank:	*Guerrilla*
Location:	*Rural Cambodia*
Conflict:	*Cambodian Civil War*

Private Afghan Army Afghan Mountains 1980

Throughout its history, the Afghan Army has demonstrated little cohesion and military application, being riven throughout its organisation by factionalism and ethnic rivalries. Despite this, it did much of the combative legwork during the Soviet Union's nine-year occupation of Afghanistan.

The structural deficiencies of the Afghan Army impacted on the standard of uniforms and equipment. Combat dress for the Afghan forces was usually a scruffy mix of grey drab trousers and shirt, which also served as parade dress, and a long greatcoat issued for winter wear. This soldier is conventionally dressed in the standard Afghan Army uniform and wears a soft peaked cap which has a neck flap serving as climate protection. Beneath his basic webbing belt is worn a curious black leather belt with a conspicuous gold buckle, and this belt-over-belt arrangement is typical of Afghan Army uniform at this time. Webbing systems were often very old, with locally made leather systems proving totally inappropriate for the wet and cold of the Afghan winter or its mountain conditions. Over this soldier's leather boots are worn a pair of canvas gaiters which have stud-reinforced black leather sections to give additional strength. A lack of up-to-date military clothing in the Afghan Army was often compounded by a similar problem in terms of weaponry. The rifle which this soldier holds, a Mosin-Nagant 7.62mm M1944 carbine, ceased production in 1950.

Date:	*1980*
Unit:	*Afghan Army*
Rank:	*Private*
Location:	*Afghan Mountains*
Conflict:	*Afghan War*

Guerrilla Mujaheddin Afghan Mountains 1980

Though the Mujaheddin's military impact was always hampered by infighting and a lack of modern equipment, their uncompromising prosecution of a terror campaign against the occupying Soviet forces in Afghanistan resulted in the withdrawal of the superpower army in 1988.

As a fighting force the Mujaheddin guerrillas of Afghanistan held significant natural advantages in their nine-year war against the Soviets. The mountainous regions of Afghanistan in the centre and north-east of the country formed a protective hinterland into which the guerrillas could disappear after operations, while the equally mountainous border with Pakistan provided another haven. Mujaheddin weapons were often in scarce supply, and rifles such as the British Lee Enfields and the Soviet AK-47/AKM were particularly desirable. However, the guerrilla pictured here holds a more common form of armament, a simple bolt-action rifle with personal adaptations. His dress is traditional Afghan civilian wear: a plain thigh-length jacket and baggy calf-length trousers, the brown waistcoat being common to the Mujaheddin. The body is wrapped in a blue sash and supplies are carried in the musette bag slung across the chest. Footwear is locally produced leather sandals. A variety of fur hats and caps are worn by the Mujaheddin.

The Mujaheddin gained a reputation as a particularly cruel enemy, and the morale of Soviet forces was steadily sapped by a deep fear of capture and the violent ambushes in mountain passes.

Date:	*1980*
Unit:	*Mujaheddin*
Rank:	*Guerrilla*
Location:	*Afghan Mountains*
Conflict:	*Afghan War*

Private Army of the Republic of Korea 1990s

Though the army of the Republic of Korea has not seen major combat since the deployment of the Capital and White Horse divisions in Vietnam, its large and advanced forces are in a constant state of readiness owing to continuing tensions with North Korea. Defensive investments made between 1980 and 1990 updated the technological capabilities of South Korean defence and made its army one of the most modern in the region.

After the Korean War, the US was the predominant military influence on all aspects of the ROK's defence, and South Korea continued to host a large US ground force. The US presence made its mark on ROK Army uniforms, and in many ways there is little to visually distinguish an ROK soldier from his US counterpart. The soldier here is in a combat dress with a camouflage type very similar to the US M81 Woodland pattern, and his similarly camouflaged headwear is the US PASGT Kevlar helmet. The climatic changes in Korea are severe, so in the 1990s ROK troops generally wore a summer uniform of denim and a winter uniform of wool, while troops in very exposed winter zones were equipped with a padded uniform and goggles to protect against snow blindness. Webbing followed US issue, the soldier here wearing a web belt, water bottle and ammunition pouch of the US ALICE system while his firearm is the 5.56mm US M16A2 assault rifle.

Date:	*1990s*
Unit:	*Army of the Republic of Korea*
Rank:	*Private*
Location:	*Korean Border*
Conflict:	*None*

South Pacific

The South Pacific is home to vast cultural diversity and the inevitable tensions which arise from this. While some nations such as Australia and New Zealand have had comparatively limited military commitments since World War II, other nations such as Indonesia and the Philippines have been locked into long-standing wars.

The South Pacific is a region of singular ethnic and geographical complexity. From the clustering islands of the Philippines to the open landmass of Australia, the South Pacific contains a diversity of cultural, social and political entities that do not always sit together in easy juxtaposition.

Nations such as the Philippines, Indonesia and Papua New Guinea experienced significant levels of civil strife, terrorism and political oppression after 1945, and though Australia and New Zealand to the far south generally spent the latter half of the twentieth century with peaceable internal relations, they did become involved in several major international conflicts. The reasons for the conflicts varied, but whatever they were, the South Pacific has entered a new millennium as a region with a solidly militaristic future.

Australia and New Zealand

At the end of the 1990s, Australia was the greatest geographical presence in the South Pacific, though as a nation with a stable political and social system its armed forces had not reached the numbers of some of its smaller neighbours. However, it did have an advanced combined forces of about 70,000 personnel. In the mid-1990s, the Army 21 Review initiated what came to be known as the Restructuring of the Army programme. As this title suggests, this programme's aims were to renew the tactical and operational qualities of the army in line with the modern western emphasis on superior mobility and firepower to offset reductions in troop numbers and financing. The programme, similar in nature to the Joint Vision 2010 in the US, saw Australia working on a similar time-scale, though its ultimate aim was what it called the Enhanced Combat Force.

In 1999, the Australian forces experienced peacekeeping duties in Indonesia, but their military pedigree since World War II had been sustained in many other roles and conflicts, often in the company of New Zealand troops. In 1950, Australia committed two infantry battalions, one fighter squadron and some naval forces, to the UN Command in the Korean War. Likewise, New Zealand contributed one artillery regiment. The performance of the individual Australian and New Zealand soldiers was commendable, despite being few in number compared to the overall UN force, and they fought valiantly at battles such as Pusan, Sariwon and Kapyong.

The Korean War was to demonstrate that the Australian Army could exercise strong capabilities in conventional warfare when required to do so, yet subsequent years would see them tested in another equally demanding role: counter-insurgency. Australian Army Training Team Vietnam (AATTV) troops were being deployed in South Vietnam as early as 1962 to bolster the effectiveness of resistance against the Viet Cong. In 1964 selective conscription was reintroduced into Australian life to cope with a perceived lack of ability to meet national threats, and by 1965 regular army units were being committed to the jungle cauldron of Vietnam. In addition, 4000 New Zealand soldiers were deployed there, and both armies showed identical levels of initiative and resilience as they did in the Korean War.

After Vietnam, the armies of Australia and New Zealand exercised themselves in a variety of mainly peacekeeping and coalition roles, including the Gulf War. One result of their broad base of experience was that both countries had excellent Special Air Service regiments with standards of training and operational competence indistinguishable from their UK counterparts.

The Pacific Islands

In 1999, Australia's main military operation was peacekeeping duties in East Timor, a country annexed by Indonesia in 1975 and consequently subject to the most appalling human rights violations which claimed the lives of around 100,000 East Timorese. In 1999, a free vote for independence was followed by days of terrible violence by pro-Jakarta militias, violence which was only stopped by the arrival of an Australian-led UN force.

Indonesia's bloody relations with East Timor illustrate a common problem in many South Pacific nations, namely the irreconcilability of multi-ethnic communities. Because of such problems, many governments tend to be authoritative in nature and invest heavily in special forces and armoured weaponry. Indonesia, for example,

181

has some 115,000 paramilitary troops as well as about 300,000 trained militia men. Yet the presence of so much ethnic diversity and political control can often create problems within the military organisation itself. In the Philippines, the militaristic rule of Ferdinand Marcos gave unprecedented power to the large Filipino Army, yet ultimately it grew dissatisfied with political interfering and in 1982 a group of officers, naming themselves the Reform the Armed Forces Movement, engineered a revolt that threw Marcos from office. This was not the end of disturbance, however, and there were some seven attempted coups against the Corazan Acquino government. The country remained unpredictable thereafter.

Throughout the late 1980s and early 1990s, the Philippines were also the site for a guerrilla war between the government and the communist New People's Army. Guerrilla war was very common in the South Pacific islands because of factors such as the legacy of independence, the presence of many militaristic governments, the difficult ethnic mix and the close proximity to the revolutionary upheavals of South East Asia. Because the armies prepared to face both large-scale civil unrest and more focused terrorist activities, there was an equal concentration in many South Pacific armies between the conventional and special forces. Indonesia, for example, not only kept the large-scale army mentioned above, but also many specialist military units falling under the category of Komando Pasukan Khusus (KPK), or Army Special Forces. The embarrassment for the West, given Indonesia's history of oppression, was that apart from the large amounts of weapons it supplied to Indonesia throughout the 1980s, the KPK were also trained at the hands of the US Army's SFOD-D, the German GSG-9 and the British, Australian and New Zealand SAS.

New Policies

By the late 1990s, like any major world region, the armies in the South Pacific varied in their levels of weaponry and equipment, though the US and Europe were the most common sources of military stock. However, most South Pacific nations had little in the way of disposable wealth, so the relatively high levels of manpower tended to be the major source of strength for those countries which couldn't invest in the best technology on the market. The major suppliers of world weaponry – especially the US, UK and western Europe – were under increasing pressure to exercise ethical foreign policies and restrict arms supplies only to those countries which intended to use them for national defence. It will be interesting to see which armies of the South Pacific will suffer under this new ethos, as the social turbulence in many of these islands makes any purchase of weaponry a potential tool of ethnic suppression and civil conflict.

◄ *An Australian infantryman on a coastal deployment. The camouflage uniform and helmet cover, plus the extensive webbing system, can be a significant burden in tropical climates.*

▼ *Australian forces are often identifiable by their distinctive items of equipment or dress, especially their standard issue assault rifle: the unusual-looking 5.56mm Steyr-Mannlicher AUG.*

Private Royal Australian Regt Kapyong 1951

During the Korean War, Australia contributed two infantry battalions, one fighter squadron and selected naval forces, to the UN resistance against North Korea. In April 1951, Australian soldiers fought part of a massive counter-attack by Chinese and Communist forces near Kapyong, an hard-fought action for which the 3rd Battalion won a US Presidential citation for bravery.

This soldier is a member of the 3rd Battalion Royal Australian Regiment. The defining mark of his national origin is the wide-brimmed slouch hat characteristic of Australian ground troops, worn with muslin puggree. British and US influences run through the rest of his outfit and equipment. The jacket and trousers are from the US M1943 combat dress and are made of a light windproof and rain-resistant material, with warmth coming from the standard Australian fatigues worn underneath and the leather gloves and thick wool scarf. The brown leather boots are worn with a pair of US-style gaiters secured by two buckle straps on each gaiter.

British Commonwealth associations come through in the webbing and the weapons. Webbing is the Australian version of the British 1937-pattern, which apart from his backpack supports two bulky ammunition pouches at the front and a 1907-pattern sword bayonet for the .303 British (Australian) Rifle No.1 Mk III. The cloth bandoliers hung across this soldier's chest would contain additional clips of ammunition for his rifle.

Date:	*1951*
Unit:	*3rd Bn Royal Australian Regiment*
Rank:	*Private*
Location:	*Near Kapyong, South Korea*
Conflict:	*Korean War*

Marine Indonesian Navy Marine Corps 1963

Indonesia found its independence from Dutch rule in 1949, but like many post-colonial states, it suffered a series of civil wars following self-rule. Between 1963 and 1966, Indonesian Marines found themselves in conflict with British and Malaysian forces during the 'Confrontation' in Borneo.

The Marines were Indonesia's most capable troops, specially trained in the amphibious warfare techniques necessary to control Indonesia's string of Pacific islands, though they suffered something of neglect as a naval force when the army took control of Indonesia with the overthrow of President Sukarno in 1965. Apart from his firearm, the Marine pictured here has a uniform almost entirely based on US models of combat dress. The helmet is the US M1-pattern steel helmet camouflaged with a fabric cover from US World War II stock. Though there are stylistic differences from the US Marine uniform of the period, the soldier's combat dress is in a US camouflage pattern of dappled brown and olive-green on a light-green base first developed for US Marines in the Pacific. The badge visible on his sleeve is the emblem of the Indonesian Marine Corps.

The 10-pouch belt and webbing is also of US origin, often worn by US airborne troops during the 1950s. Here it holds clips of 7.62mm ammunition for his Czech VZ52 rifle, a stocky weapon with the unusual feature of a permanently attached folding bayonet, which fitted into a recess in the side of the wooden stock when folded.

Date:	*1963*
Unit:	*Indonesian Marine Corps*
Rank:	*Marine*
Location:	*Borneo*
Conflict:	*Indonesian Confrontation*

Private ANZ Task Force South Vietnam 1965

The perceived threat of communist expansion from North Vietnam was not only a cause of concern for South Vietnam and the United States. Australia and New Zealand also felt their Pacific security jeopardised by developments in South East Asia and so contributed a significant ANZ Task Force to the Vietnam conflict.

The New Zealand private seen here is instantly distinguishable from an American soldier by his 7.62mm FN-FAL rifle which, alongside the Sterling 9mm submachine gun, was standard issue throughout most Commonwealth forces at that time. The bayonet for the rifle is visible on the soldier's left hip. The uniform itself is standard olive-green fatigues with epaulettes on the jacket and a single thigh pocket on the left of the trousers, as with Australian uniforms. ANZ headgear tended to be the short-brimmed olive-green bush hat based on the British pattern, while webbing was often a mix of British and US formats. Here the soldier's ammunition and ration pouches are supplemented by a haversack.

The contributions of men and equipment from countries such as Thailand, the Philippines, Australia and New Zealand peaked around the late summer of 1967 when, despite American urgings, they refused to expand their military presence. At the time public and political confidence in the Vietnam campaign began to wane as US commitment and casualties steadily grew. This was reflected in the cautious policies of America's allies.

Date:	*1967*
Unit:	*ANZ Task Force*
Rank:	*Private*
Location:	*South Vietnam*
Conflict:	*Vietnam War*

Trooper
AATTV
Vietnam 1970

The Australian Army Training Team was one of the most distinguished units operating in Vietnam. Though there were on average only 100 AATTV men in the entire Training Team, the unit finished their duties in Vietnam with four Victoria Crosses and numerous other Vietnamese and American citations, testament to the bravery and skill shown thoroughout their involvement in Vietnam.

The soldier here displays the customisation of uniform and equipment typical of special forces units. The camouflage is the distinctive 'Tiger Stripe' pattern adopted by other elite units within the US and more generally across the South Vietnamese Army. The mixture of dark and light colouration and foliage motifs was ideal for the operations characteristic of the war in Vietnam, breaking up the outline of the soldier when placed against a backdrop of dense leaves and branches. The only piece of equipment of truly Australian provenance are his boots, which are made of kangaroo hide and were standard issue for the Australian Army. Webbing is mainly the US M56 equipment, though the two ammunition pouches at the front are locally made and contain magazines for the short-barrelled 7.62mm Self Loading Rifle (SLR), in contrast to the usual US M16 rifle carried by most Allied troops.

Further offensive or defensive equipment here includes two M8 smoke grenades strapped to his chest and, slung over his left shoulder, a bag for carrying demolition explosives.

Date:	*1970*
Unit:	*Australian Army Training Team*
Rank:	*Trooper*
Location:	*Vietnamese Jungle*
Conflict:	*Vietnam War*

Trooper Australian SAS Philippines 1980s

The Australian SAS was formed in 1957 and has since then earned a distinguished combat record in places such as Brunei and Vietnam. Like the British SAS, their standards of training and toughness are exemplary.

The similarities to the British SAS extend to the style of uniform and insignia worn by the Australian soldiers. Though the Australian SAS wear the standard Australian camouflage uniform, they share with their UK counterpart the sand-coloured beret and the SAS badge with the 'Who Dares Wins' motto. Parachute wings are also frequently worn on the right sleeve and many Australian SAS are highly trained in parachute deployment techniques. This soldier, however, displays no markings or insignia to retain his operational anonymity. Dressed entirely in a camouflage combat suit, he has a sweatrag wrapped around his head so that perspiration droplets do not interfere with his aim.

The Australian SAS tend to mix the best, or most appropriate, US and British equipment. This is illustrated here in the mixing of the US 1967-pattern web belt with a British Bergen rucksack, the latter camouflaged in sympathy with the uniform. The weapon is the US 5.56mm M16A1, the later A2 version having a heavier barrel and a deflector near the ejection port to stop left-handed firers being hit by expended bullet casings.

Date:	*1980s*
Unit:	*Australian SAS*
Rank:	*Trooper*
Location:	*Philippines*
Conflict:	*Unknown*

China

With the Cold War split of East and West now dissolved, China enters the new millennium as one of the world's few remaining communist countries. Its investment in military technology remains high in both conventional and strategic weaponry, and it is fast becoming a superpower army in its own right.

In 1999, China celebrated its 50th anniversary as a communist state. It did so with a parade of typically impressive scale, colour and energy, a parade which not only demonstrated China's continuing bond to Marxist ideology, but also showed off the full extent of its growing military arsenal. Alongside the 500,000 soldiers marching through Tiananmen Square in front of the Chinese leader, Jiang Zemin, were numerous tanks, amphibious vehicles, towed and self-propelled artillery pieces, anti-aircraft and anti-ship missiles and fighter jets. Yet causing most concern to international observers were the new Dong Feng 31 intercontinental ballistic missiles, systems which could deliver a 250-kilotonne nuclear warhead as far as the north-west coast of the United States and the westernmost reaches of Europe.

Despite the anachronistic feel that such parades naturally carry, the 50th anniversary celebrations put China back at the forefront of international defence issues. Its new missile systems, while not directly constituting a threat, at least issued a warning that Chinese power is as relevant today as it was in 1949.

The People's Republic of China was born out of the principles of 'People's War'. With the end of World War II, Mao Tse-Tung's communist People's Liberation Army (PLA) set about destabilising the Nationalist government of Chiang Kai-Shek through a sequenced strategy of attrition then open warfare. This strategy had three phases: 1) The creation of a social and logistical support structure; 2) Insistent and prolonged guerrilla warfare aimed at weakening opposing forces; 3) Finally, when the time was right, open warfare using conventional tactics to defeat the enemy. As the 50th anniversary indicated, this strategy brought success: Peking was captured by the communists in October 1949. The significance of the People's War was more than just its initial revolutionary impact. In fact, the concepts of People's War were enshrined as China's main military doctrine from the early 1950s to the mid-1970s, and even today it still has an important role in Chinese strategic thought. People's War, with its reliance upon patient communal action, the resources of the individual, and mobility, was very much in line with the communist ideals of unity and action lying in the hands of the many, though events from 1950 started to put some severe dents in this credo.

The Korean War brought China into direct conflict with a US-dominated UN army fighting against the expansionism of communist North Korea. Chinese soldiers, fresh from revolutionary war, did have the major advantage of experience over their opponents, but this was mostly expressed through courage, resilience and tactical mobility. Such qualities, though bringing the PLA some initial success, soon came into contact with the storm of UN firepower, and the losses in PLA lives were truly dreadful (about 900,000 killed by 1953). Such an unequal death toll forced the PLA to adopt more conventional strategies using artillery and other heavy weaponry, with the recognition that technology could triumph over sheer human will on the battlefield.

Modernisation

It was this recognition, as well as a potentially hostile break in relations with the Soviet Union, that pushed China towards a greater investment in nuclear weapons research in the 1960s. The ideological constraints of People's War tended to keep PLA soldiers badly equipped and armed, and the diversion of even more funds towards nuclear weapons only accentuated this situation. PLA footsoldiers were generally armed with either Soviet weapons or Chinese copies, weapons which usually lagged behind those of most other great world armies at the time. Even at the end of the 1990s, antiquated weaponry is still common amongst the PLA, yet since the beginning of the decade, with China's widening commercial involvements, technological sophistication started to creep into its conventional firepower as well as its strategic missile systems.

The seeds of this technological advance were sown in the late 1970s, when China embarked upon a major modernisation programme within its armed forces. On an ideological level, this modernisation involved an updating of People's War into 'People's War under modern conditions'. This new strategic rule emphasised more conventional defence strategies based on firepower and immediate response to threat, rather than long campaigns of guerrilla warfare, and its rather open-ended formulation allowed the PLA to adapt to a conflict and not necessarily follow strict doctrinal rules. The modernisation programme also included an emphasis on greater liaison between civilian research and military technology, an enhanced training of PLA soldiers in new weaponry and tactics, and also a new look to uniforms and insignia.

Rank Opposition

During the 1950s, China's unswerving commitment to the abolition of social status led to the removal of a rank system within the Chinese forces. Simple divisions remained which distinguished between various levels of experience, but by 1984 it was becoming apparent to all in government that the rank system was essential not only for discipline but also for combat effectiveness, as China's conflict on the Sino-Vietnamese border had proved in 1979. The 1984 Military Service Law ordered the reintroduction of ranks and following this was a new style uniform. Earlier PLA uniforms tended towards simple olive-green or khaki fatigues with few insignia. The new uniform for ground forces was a visored cap with olive-green summer fatigues and dark-blue winter fatigues issued with a new collar insignia and shoulder boards. The cap motif was five stars and ideographs denoting the date of the Nanchang Uprising (1 August 1927) all surrounded by images of wheat ears and cog wheels. The introduction of these uniforms brought greater distinction between ranks and units and took the PLA's appearance away from a confusing uniformity.

China's position in international relations as it enters the twenty-first century is awkward. On the one hand, its government has opened greater economic connections with the west, especially with its old enemy, the United States. Yet the massacre of student demonstrators in Tiananmen Square in 1989, the test firing of ballistic missiles across Taiwan and the return of Hong Kong to Chinese rule has kept these growing connections under an increasing tension. Whatever the size or nature of a nation's military force, its acquisition of nuclear weaponry dramatically alters the political balance of the region to which it belongs, as the world experienced in the case of India and Pakistan in the late 1990s. The Dong Feng 31 missile which was paraded during the Chinese anniversary celebrations in 1999 was far from the end of China's development of strategic rocketry. Already the Dong Feng 41 was under development with an almost global range of 12,070km (7500 miles). The production of such weapons may be little more than technological posturing, but with a long history of tensions between China and Russia, Taiwan and other South-East Asian neighbours, such military expansion is bound to produce worldwide anxieties for the future.

▶ *Archaic-looking PLA soldiers provide a memorable image of communist military dress. Between the 1950s and 1984, China abolished the rank system, which caused great confusion.*

Guerrilla Chinese Communist Forces 1945

In 1945, the communist forces under Mao Tse-Tung had at their disposal some 880,000 regular troops and around 500,000 guerrilla soldiers. The latter were vital to Mao Tse-Tung's concept of 'People's War', especially in wearing down nationalist resistance prior to the initiation of conventional war between the respective armies.

All the elements of this soldier's uniform are locally produced with most of the clothes being of traditional Chinese peasant dress. One of the greatest problems suffered by the guerrilla soldiers in their fight against the nationalists was the dire lack of equipment and weaponry, especially in the immediate aftermath of World War II when the resources of the Pacific War were no longer available to them. This situation was partly remedied by the Soviet Union's major contribution of captured Japanese arms in 1946 and the PLA's continuing capture of nationalist guns. This soldier is carrying a simple bolt-action Chinese rifle. The most distinctive part of his outfit is his 'webbing', which consists of simple cotton or canvas bandoliers for ammunition around his chest and waist, while slung around his neck is a holder for two stick grenades. Once the war expanded into a conventional conflict, many guerrillas changed their appearance for that of the regular People's Liberation Army.

In 1945, the communist guerrillas generally operated in small teams of less than 20 and fought an energetic war of attrition against the nationalist strongholds in southern China.

Date:	*1945*
Unit:	*Chinese Communist Forces*
Rank:	*Guerrilla*
Location:	*Southern China*
Conflict:	*Chinese Civil War*

Private Chinese Communist Army 1945

Perhaps the most distinctive feature of this Communist infantryman is his gun. Despite its rather imbalanced appearance, the 9mm United Defense Model 42 was a superior weapon with very high, though expensive, standards of manufacture and reliability. Only 15,000 of these firearms were produced between 1938 and 1943, and this soldier possesses one of the few which must have reached China, most likely via the Pacific theatres of World War II.

Such a weapon must have been a distinct exception to the combat equipment of the communist forces, as from 1945 most communist troops were equipped with either Soviet-supplied Japanese weapons or captured nationalist firearms. The leather pouches for the M42's 20-round magazines are easily identified by their length in contrast to the shorter pouches which would have held pistol ammunition or rifle clips. The khaki uniform worn by this communist soldier here is typical of Chinese combat dress as a whole, both Communist and Nationalist, with especially archaic features such as the knee-length woollen puttees.

By 1946 the communist forces would have found the label People's Liberation Army (PLA). Their unified efforts to destroy the less-organised Nationalist Army started to pay off between 1947 and 1948, when a series of offensive victories, the acquisition of large amounts of Nationalist arms and increasing popular support throughout China led inevitably to the establishment of a communist state.

Date:	*1945*
Unit:	*Chinese Communist Army*
Rank:	*Private*
Location:	*Northern China*
Conflict:	*Chinese Civil War*

India & Pakistan

India and Pakistan have been locked in conflict and aggression from the very moment that the British ended their rule over the Indian subcontinent in 1947. The Indian and Pakistani armies thus remain in a constant state of readiness for war, and both countries have now developed their own nuclear arsenals.

India & Pakistan

In October 1999, a military coup took place in Pakistan. The purpose and objectives of this (seemingly successful) overthrow were initially unclear, yet Pakistan's status as a new nuclear nation in a volatile region made international concern guaranteed, for these were sensitive times in the Indian sub-continent. Both India and Pakistan were in possession of nuclear weapons, and with a long history of war and aggression between the two nations, the use of such weapons was an actual rather than theoretical threat.

India achieved independence from Britain in 1947 after a long period of violent and non-violent direct action against the colonial forces. However, it was born into partition rather than unity, as the separate Muslim nation of Pakistan was created in the north to handle the Hindu and Muslim schisms that had dogged India's internal relations for centuries. Yet the partition did most things except secure peace. India and Pakistan are complex nations, with an almost uncountable variety of religious and ethnic groups that are far from unified within national borders. In addition, disputed territories would remain, especially the region of Kashmir which was partitioned shortly after independence but was a source of conflict from that point onwards. Indeed, concerns about Indo-Pakistan relations revolved around the resumption of fighting in Kashmir in 1999.

The first Indo-Pakistan war (1947–48) flared into life alongside India's early, tottering steps into independence. In the Indian-controlled state of Jammu and Kashmir (to give it its full name), tribes favouring a Muslim Kashmir attacked Indian forces in the north-west of the territory. The Indian forces retaliated successfully, but the conflict escalated, with Pakistan committing its conventional forces through fear that its own nation was under threat. The conflict was eventually resolved through UN brokerage and Kashmir was accordingly partitioned, but not before India and Pakistan had suffered combined losses of more than 3000 men.

Though the Kashmir issue remained politically and militarily volatile, it was to take until 1965 before the second Indo-Pakistan war exploded. From 5 August 1965, fighting broke out in the Indian sector of Kashmir between Muslim guerrillas sponsored by Pakistan and the Indian Army. What began as a local military action soon expanded into an undeclared war as Indian and Pakistani conventional forces met in combat around 14 August. Strategic advantage alternated from one side to the other with every attack and counter-attack, and the war saw both armies making heavy deployments of armour and also airpower to strike deep into each other's territory. Despite India's capture of positions 8km (5 miles) inside Pakistani territory, by mid-September of that year, the war had degenerated into a stalemate, and it ended on 23 September, again with UN arbitration. This war was even more costly than the first: 3000 Indian deaths and 3800 Pakistani deaths.

The third and final major war between Pakistan and India came in 1971, but unlike the first two, its cause was not Kashmir but Pakistan itself. On independence Pakistan was divided between geographically separate east and west regions. However, in 1970 East Pakistan raised growing demands for independence from its western counterpart, demands which were militarily suppressed in March 1971.

The New State of Bangladesh

This conflict in itself was bloody, leaving many thousands of East Pakistani civilians dead, some 10 million refugees pouring into West Bengal, and importantly, many Pakistani Army soldiers crossing the lines to join East Pakistan forces. India saw its chance. After drawing up a proposal for an independent East Pakistan, to be Bangladesh, India started to train and equip East Pakistani fighters while also signing a mutual protection pact with the Soviet Union to enhance its defensive muscle. For Pakistan this was too much, and on 3 December 1971 it started air attacks on Indian airbases in the west. India replied in kind and, as the air war gathered momentum, invaded East Pakistan with massed forces. India's tactics in this war had changed from its rather lumbering use of the army in previous conflicts. This time it used more mobile rapid-deployment tactics to punch a hole in the Pakistani formations and by 16 December East Pakistan was in Indian hands. The fighting in the west was also ferocious, including a massive tank battle in Kashmir and over 4000 combat sorties by the Indian Air Force. By now, Pakistan's heavy losses began to tell and it eventually surrendered East Pakistan as the new state of Bangladesh.

197

Since the third Indo-Pakistani war, military aggression between the two countries simmered in the background, with occasional artillery and troop engagements in the Kashmiri mountains, engagements which saw an intensification in the 1990s. However, more general religious violence continued in many forms throughout the Indian sub-continent.

India's history of war since 1945 is not just that of its problems with Pakistan. In 1962 it also fought a major war with China over other disputed territories in the north of the country. China attacked India on 20 October 1962 with nine divisions and though India put up a spirited defence in places, its forces were almost completely dominated by the Chinese. By 21 November all the disputed territories were in the hands of the Chinese. The defeat was a hard one for the Indian Army, and tensions with China did not start to subside until talks were instigated in 1994.

Modern Armies

As one would expect, given the history of their region, the Indian and Pakistani armies received heavy investment and stood as two of the world's more advanced military forces. Both armies emerged out of their British colonial heritage, the legacy of this being the khaki uniforms, rank insignia, British webbing systems and military etiquette that tend to prevail amongst their land forces. However, this influence naturally started to wane after independence, especially in India where a career in the armed forces was made more democratically accessible to those who were previously restricted on account of their religious or social background.

India, as the wealthier of the two countries, despite its prevalent poverty had the means to purchase advanced weaponry. From 1965, the Indian army started a rapid period of modernisation, which meant a greater acquisition of superior weaponry which supported its more modern tactics. In 1994, defence spending was just

under 5 per cent of GDP and, apart from acquiring high-quality foreign weaponry, it also took to manufacturing more armaments in India itself. With over 3400 main battle tanks, about 900,000 men and 4000 towed artillery pieces, India's strength became considerable. Pakistan's resources did not approach India's, and it had always struggled against being under-equipped and undermanned, particularly in the early decades after independence when trained Muslim soldiers were especially scarce. However, the ongoing wars over Kashmir prompted rapid development and, despite continuing shortages of equipment, the Pakistani Army performed well in combat.

War Without End

Of course, once both India and Pakistan were equipped with nuclear weapons, their conventional armouries were less relevant to the overall strategic picture. The concern for many foreign nations became that the ease with which conventional forces had been committed in the past could be transferred to nuclear weapons in the future. Nuclear weapons, however, may make both sides reluctant to open any sort of hostilities in the future, though with the 1999 coup in Pakistan, we have few assurances.

◀ *Pakistani sailors on parade not only present a demonstration of military strength for Pakistani citizens, but also act as part of the continual sabre-rattling that occurs with their neighbour.*

▼ *Indian soldiers prepare a mortar emplacement during the conflict in East Pakistan during 1971. India used new tactics to snatch a conclusive victory over the Pakistani forces.*

Private Azad Kashmir Army Kashmir 1950

The Azad ('Free') Kashmir Army were a small military force dedicated to the overthrow of Hindu rule in the mainly Muslim nation of Kashmir following the partition of India in 1947. Sponsored by Pakistan in terms of equipment and training, they did not lack a strong fighting spirit, but ultimately they were politically and militarily submerged in the overall strategic picture of the Indian and Pakistani states.

The Azad Kashmir soldiers would dress in whatever was available, civilian or military. Yet with increasing supplies of Pakistani equipment flowing across the border from late 1947, their uniforms are frequently made up of elements of Pakistani military dress. This soldier's uniform is similar to the cavalry uniforms of the Indian Army before independence. Pakistan itself obtained much of its equipment from the Indian Army after the division of India and this would then filter through to the Azad Kashmir. The long khaki tunic and heavy-looking drill trousers would have provided a reasonable measure of cold protection in the high altitudes of the Kashmiri mountains and this soldier wears a military beret as headgear, though many Azad Kashmir soldiers are to be seen in the muslim turban.

The soldier's weapon, like that of much of the Pakistani Army, is the British bolt-action .303 Lee Enfield Mk III rifle, and instead of carrying his ammunition in pouches, he has it slung around his neck in a bandolier.

Date:	*1950*
Unit:	*Azad Kashmir Army*
Rank:	*Private*
Location:	*Kashmir*
Conflict:	*Kashmir Independence War*

Lance Corporal Indian Army Kashmir 1965

The Indo-Pakistan war of 1965 was just one of several wars in the long-standing tensions between India and Pakistan. Though the situation was brought under control through Western brokerage, the stand-off over Kashmir was still in evidence at the end of the 1990s, and it remains an issue of contention.

By his emphatically British uniform, this lance corporal of the Indian Army testifies to India's past involvement with Britain's colonial armed forces. The rifle he carries, the .303 calibre Lee Enfield No.1 Mk III, was the veteran rifle of the British and Commonwealth forces and is here seen with a 1907-pattern bayonet attached. Over the olive-green uniform is worn British 1937-pattern webbing, a simple webbing system which here carries two pouches and a bayonet frog on the left hip. A small haversack and water bottle are fitted around the back, hanging from between the ends of the shoulder straps and short belt attachments. The soldier's devotion to the Sikh religion is immediately identified by his turban, coloured olive-green to match the uniform. The red band just visible beneath the turban is known as a 'fifty' after the fiftieth turn of the turban in fitting. A steel band is worn around his right wrist as a traditional piece of Sikh jewellery.

India's conflict with Pakistan in 1965 proved to be a turning point for the Indian armed forces, with ethnic and social elitism being reduced in army society and an increase in the effective use of tactics and equipment on the battlefield.

Date:	*1965*
Unit:	*Indian Army*
Rank:	*Lance Corporal*
Location:	*Kashmir*
Conflict:	*Indo-Pakistani War*

201

Falklands War

The Cold War politics of Central America dominated the skyline of Latin American international relations, but at the other end of the continent a war of different motivation was fought in 1982. The Falklands (Malvinas) War was a symptom of South America's growing military confidence, as Argentina invaded the Falkland Islands, secure in the belief that its on-paper military superiority would withstand any British return of force. By the time the British forces had recaptured the islands, that security was shattered, and the conflict illustrated that in terms of conventional warfare, South America was still weak in trained manpower, tactics and the application of high-tech weaponry (though the Argentine use of anti-shipping missiles was to prove particularly devastating for the British Royal Navy).

Much of Latin America has large conventional armies, and frictions such as Venezuela's frontier dispute with Columbia in 1988 and Chile's long-standing tensions with Bolivia, Peru and Argentina ensured that large armies were maintained. Yet prevailing political insecurity keeps most Latin American armies involved with policing or counter-insurgency duties against frequently disorganised guerrilla armies, and this deprived them of the training in conventional warfare. However, it must be said that wars like that which occurred in the Falklands are rare occurrences for Latin America, so their forces serve them well in the capacities for which they are most often needed.

The military situation in Latin America as a whole in the 1990s was more peaceable than it had been for many years, so it gave little surprise to see defence budgets in many nations steadily shrinking. Countries like Bolivia, El Salvador and Columbia had military expenditure pushed extremely high during periods of civil conflict, and though expenditure was still proportionately large compared to many other nations, it was steadily declining by

◀ *Troops in El Salvador undergo training in the use of a mortar. El Salvador's civil war, which lasted over a decade in the 1970s and 1980s, would give most men a regular taste of combat.*

▲ *An Argentine soldier uses his equipment to cook up a meal in cold conditions during the Argentine occupation of the Falkland Islands in April and May 1982.*

the end of the twentieth century. In addition, more South American armies were stepping out from under the US, Soviet or European umbrellas to start building up their own arms industries. Chile, for instance, made only basic infantry weaponry until the 1970s, when it underwent a modernisation programme and started to produce more advanced firearms and, by 1994, armoured vehicles. Brazil is also active in the manufacture of arms and military equipment.

However, each nation in Latin America has its own specific policy for defence spending. US and European equipment was still very prevalent throughout the continent and, as Cold War issues lessened, this looked as it might well become more so as western countries developed new arms markets. Yet Latin America remained socially precarious in many places, and as long as traditions of military rule and the efficacy of the coup are in place in the future, its armies will no doubt find themselves in use.

Guerrilla Cuban Revolutionaries Havana 1959

Equipping a revolutionary army is a process that snowballs: the greater the military successes on the battlefield, the more equipment is captured from the enemy, and the more likely the army is to win, and thus the cycle begins again. The Cuban revolutionaries who sought to and eventually succeeded in overthrowing the government of Fulgencio Batista in the 1950s had to operate on such a principle, though some considerable defeats in the field also left them short of military essentials.

This Cuban rebel has kitted himself out in mainly US clothing and equipment which would have been taken from the US-sponsored soldiers backing the Cuban Government. His zippered jacket is of civilian origin, but the herringbone twill uniform underneath is the US combat dress typically worn by the US Marines during the latter stages of World War II and by some troops during the Korean War. The webbing belt is also of US issue, identifiable by the small ammunition pouches generally used for the M1 Garand rifle but here used for the same calibre (.30in) M1903 Springfield, which was in production in the US in various versions up until 1965.

Despite all the US features of this man's dress, he has introduced custom elements which identify him instantly as a rebel soldier. Berets were a prevalent form of revolutionary headgear throughout this period, and the large patch on his jacket sleeve shows his allegiance to a new Cuban identity.

Date:	*1959*
Unit:	*Cuban Revolutionaries*
Rank:	*Guerrilla*
Location:	*Havana*
Conflict:	*Cuban Civil War*

Private
Cuban Army
Angola 1976

During Angola's immediate independence from Portuguese rule in 1975, Cuba sent some 11,000 troops to bolster the dominant MPLA communist party against a hostile mix of, amongst others, FNLA, UNITA, Zairean and South African forces. Cuba's initial commitment was small and poorly armed, but by 1976 a heavier commitment of Cuban manpower and Soviet heavy weapons meant that resistance to the MPLA was effectively crushed and communist influence maintained in southern Africa.

Soviet materials and weaponry were the key to Cuban operations in Angola, and the soldier pictured here shows the dependency very clearly. The Soviet-supplied 7.62mm AKM assault rifle was the predominant firearm for Cuban soldiers and communist forces around the world, and this soldier wears the standard ammunition pouch on his belt to hold the AKM's 30-round magazine. Acting as a bayonet for his AKM is a survival knife attached to his Cuban-made web belt. The hilt and scabbard of the knife are insulated so that the knife can also be used as a wire cutter. The rest of his uniform is a simple olive-green set of fatigues of indeterminate origin, though most likely they are of Cuban manufacture.

The Cuban forces maintained a growing presence in the Angolan region even after the immediate defeat of opponents in 1976. They also intervened in Ethiopean affairs in the 1970s during Eritrea's struggle for independence.

Date:	*1976*
Unit:	*Cuban Army*
Rank:	*Private*
Location:	*Angola*
Conflict:	*Angolan Civil War*

Private Salvadorean Army El Salvador 1980

Apart from his West German 7.62mm G3A3 rifle, this infantryman of the Salvadorean Army is dressed in equipment of mainly US origin, indicative of the heavy US support given to the government forces in El Salvador's long-running civil war – a conflict that was seen to threaten the stability of the United States' 'backyard'.

Helmet, belt, webbing and boots are all of US Army stock. The headgear is the classic M1 steel helmet and the webbing is the US M1943 pattern, though the belt belongs to the later M1956 load-carrying equipment. To suit the hot and humid conditions of El Salvador, this soldier wears tropical boots which are a mix of green nylon and black leather, again of US origin and the same type as worn by US soldiers in Vietnam. The G3A3 rifle which this soldier holds was, and is, one of the most common military firearms in Latin America and across the globe, being used by some 60 armies throughout the world. The infantry-man's webbing is adapted from US to El Salvadorean use, with the ammunition pouches holding the G3A3's larger 7.62mm ammunition rather than the 5.56mm magazines of the M16 assault rifle, another common weapon.

From the end of 1980, the El Salvadorean Army's typical role was that of counter-insurgency in support of the government of Napoleón Duarte, a role that saw a tremendous cost in human life despite the substantial amounts of US military aid.

Date:	*1980*
Unit:	*El Salvadorean Ar*
Rank:	*Private*
Location:	*Rural El Salva r*
Conflict:	*El Salvador Civil War*

Senior Sergeant Argentine Marines East Falkland 1982

On 2 April 1982, Argentine Marines of the 2nd Marine Fleet Force led a brief and successful invasion of East Falkland. The 52-day conflict which followed saw the 601 and 602 Marine companies playing a pivotal role in resisting the advancing soldiers of the British Task Force in ferocious fighting on the Falklands' rugged terrain.

Uniforms for all forces on the Falklands had to be capable of protecting against the islands' extreme weather conditions. This Argentine NCO shows a high standard of weather-proof clothing, as was common in the more prestigious Marine units. Over his standard uniform, he wears a padded and hooded parka jacket with a zipped front, snap-fastened fly and woollen cuffs. The jacket displays the red chevrons of a Senior Sergeant, while the blue-and-white patch above the rank indicates nationality.

US equipment was prevalent in Argentine forces. The sergeant's headgear is the US M1 helmet with a camouflaged cover. The web belt is also of US manufacture with two ammunition pouches at the front. Further ammunition is carried in two bandoliers over the shoulders and the personal weapon in this case is a folding-stock version of the 7.62mm FN-FAL rifle. Being so close to the Antarctic, the goggles worn by most Argentine soldiers would have been a useful piece of equipment to protect eyes against freezing weather, though the pink- or amber-tinted lenses may have also helped enhance vision in the prevailing low-light conditions.

	June 1982
Unit:	*Argentine Marines*
Rank:	*Senior Sergeant*
Location:	*East Falkland*
Conflict:	*Falklands War*

Marine Argentinian Marine Commandos 1982

Were it not for his weaponry, this soldier of the Argentinian Marine Commandos (*Buzo Tactico*) could be a civilian hiker or mountaineer. Yet his clothing is based around the South Atlantic climate experienced in the Falklands War and would have provided him with a good level of heat retention and waterproofing in the cold conditions.

Though the Buzo Tactico, as a Special Forces unit, would have selected the best clothing and equipment for the job in hand, the outfit here was fairly standard amongst their land-based units during the brief Falklands conflict. The dark-blue woollen cap was almost standard wear for Argentine Special Forces at this time, and the thick jumper, padded anorak and trousers and high combat boots were generally sensible operational clothing for the expected weather conditions. Supplies are carried on the three-pocket rucksack and underneath that is a leather pouch which would house fresh magazines for his British 9mm L34A1 Sterling submachine gun. This weapon is the silenced version of the L2A3 Sterling, the standard submachine gun of the British Army in the 1980s. His firepower is increased by a 9mm Browning pistol, worn in a leather holster on his hip.

Though they did illustrate some degree of training and initiative, the Buzo Tactico on the Falklands were let down by poor intelligence-gathering and tactical outmanoeuvring by the British forces, and their contribution to the overall campaign was very limited compared to their British equivalents.

Date:	*April 1982*
Unit:	*Buzo Tactico*
Rank:	*Marine*
Location:	*Port Stanley*
Conflict:	*Falklands War*

Webbing & Equipment

As military technology advances, soldiers frequently find themselves having to transport more and more equipment onto the battlefield. Consequently, systems for carrying equipment have had to keep pace, and give each soldier a comfortable, strong and easily accessible method of supporting and deploying the tools of survival and war.

In 1965, a typical US Marine on a medium- to long-range operation in Vietnam would have required formidable stamina as well as combat skills. The list of the equipment he may have personally had to carry could include multiple water bottles, an entrenching tool, four pouches full of ammunition, medical packs, a fighting knife, two bags containing Claymore anti-personnel mines, a firearm weighing up to 11kg (24.5lbs) (M60), a backpack containing all his living essentials, bedding roll, waterproofs and a flak jacket, all of which had to be carried through the stifling Vietnamese heat. This exhausting burden suggests an important truth about any soldier's uniform: the way his equipment is carried is as important as the equipment itself.

Systems of webbing (i.e. the belts, straps and pouches used to carry equipment as opposed to the webbing material itself) produced since 1945 were as diverse as uniforms themselves. Yet just as uniforms saw something of a global standardisation after the end of World War II, so webbing systems also gathered around certain popular configurations. Every country's webbing system varies, but certain models have become tremendously influential throughout the world. The US, UK, Soviet Union and China in particular have almost acted as the world's stockists in load-carrying supplies and their webbing has made an appearance in almost all conflicts fought since 1945.

Webbing Designs

The US pushed webbing design further than any other nation in the twentieth century, but its early M1910 and M1956 patterns were worn by soldiers from Korea to South America. The UK gave the world the 1944- and 1958-pattern webbing systems which, apart from equipping their own army, also equipped many other forces as distinct as the Arab Legion and the Indian Army. Soviet webbing appeared outside of the Soviet Bloc in places such as the Middle East and Cuba, while the distinctive Chinese 'ChiCom' ammunition pouches found applications from Africa to Vietnam. The global prevalence of certain styles of webbing should not mask the fact that many countries did not import the original webbing systems but simply copied them, with local alterations.

Yet the influence of popular load-carrying systems established the tendency for webbing to use a simple belt and shoulder-strap configuration with several pouches and fittings for essential equipment and a space to carry a backpack.

However, the popularity of specific types did not stop major advances in webbing design. One of the biggest steps in terms of materials accompanied the production of the US M1967 Modernized Load-Carrying Equipment (LCE). Prior to this system, webbing tended to be made out of webbing material and cotton duck, which have a tendency towards dry rot and mildew, and a high absorbency of water. The M1967 Load-Carrying Equipment (LCE) used nylon as its primary material. Nylon is not only lightweight and immensely strong, but it also resists mildew and water absorption and is incredibly hard-wearing.

◀ *The soldier's burden. A British infantryman carries an extensive pack and webbing system which would enable him to survive and fight for long periods away from supply centres.*

Webbing & Equipment

With the M1967 webbing, nylon became the ideal standard material for load-carrying equipment. In terms of design, the M1967 LCE continued the trend set by the earlier M1956 system of using very broad shoulder straps to disperse as much weight as possible across the soldier's shoulders, which led to another major innovation in webbing. Development began in 1984 on the Integrated Individual Fighting System (IIFS), an advanced LCE which pursued the idea of the Individual Tactical Load Bearing Vest (ITLBV). As its name suggests, this was a vest-type system which had the pouches built into broad panels and was worn like an additional piece of clothing. The IIFS became a standard issue throughout the US due to its superior comfort and its excellent distribution of weight over the entire torso rather than just the shoulders. Variations on these combat vests became popular with special forces, particularly those which specialised in urban warfare where close-fitting LCE was essential for fighting in confined spaces. Such advanced vest-type LCEs are still rare, however, and for many armies with limited budgets more traditional styles of webbing remained perfectly adequate and useable.

Despite a general lightening of the individual components which a modern soldier carries, there is no indication that the overall weight carried is any less burdensome from that of earlier times (if anything the demands could be even greater, particularly with modern anti-tank missile systems). The challenge for those who design infantry equipment is to push the operational limits of each soldier while recognising that he or she is still bound by physical structure.

▼ *These heavily-armed West German soldiers are wearing combat order webbing, the priority being given to weaponry, ammunition and mobility rather than long-range endurance.*

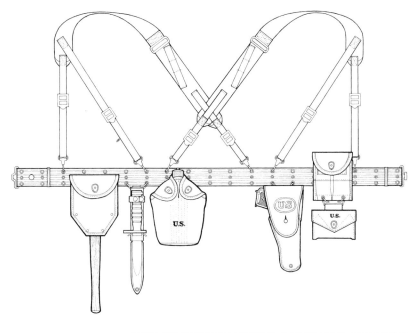

Date:	1951
Location:	Korea

US Infantryman's M1910 Webbing

The Improved M1910 webbing featured here is a simple system for transporting essential fighting gear, though in actual combat the soldier would probably be carrying far more ammunition pouches than the one shown.

The ammunition pouch is situated to the right on the M1936 web belt and would hold one 15-round magazine for a US .30 M1 carbine. Suspended beneath this pouch is a small M1942 first-aid pack. Next to the ammunition is a .45 Colt M1911 automatic pistol in a leather holster, standard issue for men with carbines. Crossing to the left of the belt, the three items there are a black enamelled water canteen in an M1910 cover, an M4 bayonet and an M1943 entrenching tool and carrier. Most US infantry in Korea would actually be wearing the standard multi-pouch rifleman's webbing when engaged in combat operations.

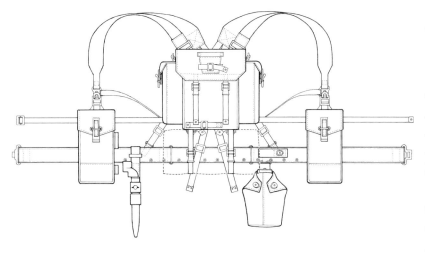

Date:	1956
Location:	Suez, Egypt

British Paratrooper 1944-Pattern Webbing

This diagram illustrates the 1944-pattern webbing in its full Battle Order, and its light weight made it a good system for use during parachute drops such as those undertaken by the British paratroopers at Suez.

The three-piece belt and shoulder-straps held the backpack and pouches firmly to the wearer's back, though the middle strap was often omitted. In the centre is a three-compartment backpack with a waterproof central section strap and a buckle on the flap that could be used to secure an entrenching tool. Below the haversack were straps for fitting a bedding roll (here indicated in outline). Two ammunition pouches for a 9mm Mark V Sten submachine gun frame a Number 9 bayonet and a water bottle. The strap above the water bottle could be used to secure a rifle butt when hung over the right shoulder.

US M1956 Load-Carrying Equipment

The M1956 load-carrying equipment was the first of a new generation of webbing systems developed by the US forces, and was the standard for troops during the Vietnam War until the advent of the M1967 system.

The basic components of the M1956 were a pistol belt (with a quick release buckle), carrying suspenders, a first aid or compass pouch, an entrenching-tool carrier, a combat field pack, a canteen cover and a sleeping-bag carrier. Here the configuration generally follows those lines with the substitution of another water bottle in place of the entrenching tool, a typical replacement for the hot operating climate of Vietnam. The M7 bayonet on the left is for the M16 rifle. The M1956 pack was superseded by the M1961 pack which had a more substantial flap and a rubberised edge to the opening.

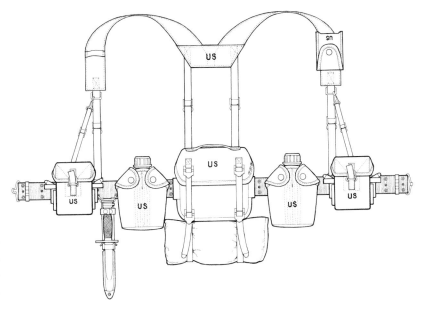

Date:	1966
Location:	Vietnam

Viet Cong Load-Carrying Equipment

The sheer volume of equipment presented here indicates both the length of time that Viet Cong guerrillas would have to operate in the field and the physical stamina demanded of these resourceful soldiers.

At the bottom on the far left is a simple musette bag holding either rations or weaponry. This bag, like the Chinese water bottle on the opposite side, would be hung as separate items over the shoulders. Between them is a belt with communist star buckle, on which there is a canvas holder for two NVA stick grenades and another small storage pouch, perhaps for first aid. Fitted centrally around the back and chest is the 10-pouch ammunition belt, storing 200 rounds for the Soviet SKS rifle. The rest of his or her equipment would be stored in the Vietnamese-produced pack at the top of the illustration.

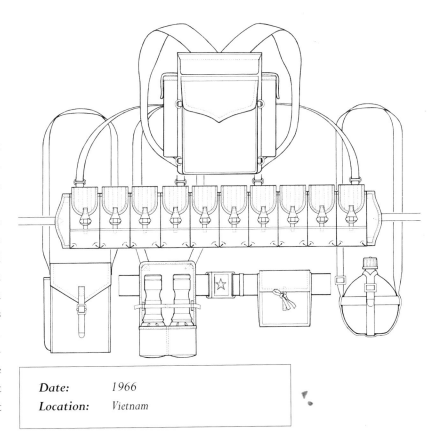

Date:	1966
Location:	Vietnam

Gurkha Rifleman's 1944-Pattern Webbing

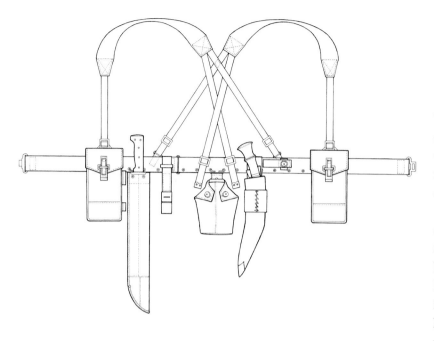

Though the 1944-pattern webbing had been superseded by the 1958-pattern, the 7th Gurkha Rifles operating in Borneo in 1966 retained the 1944-pattern which was, after all, designed for jungle combat.

This is Battle Order adapted for operating in conditions of dense foliage. The much-feared kukri fighting knife is the item that defines this kit as belonging to a Gurkha. Supplementing the kukri is a long machete for clearing vegetation. Two ammunition pouches are worn in the usual location over the hips, and they would have carried the 20- or 30-round magazines for the 5.56mm M16A1 rifle. Standard equipment on this webbing was the 1944-pattern aluminium water bottle and the loop (to the right of the kukri) for supporting the butt of a slung rifle. To the immediate right of the machete is a bayonet frog.

Date:	1966
Location:	Borneo

US Special Forces Load-Carrying Eqpt

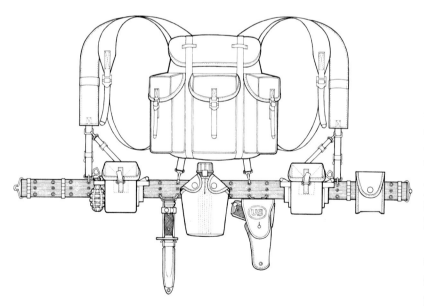

Special Forces soldiers in Vietnam had no standard configuration of webbing, using whatever equipment was necessary. Here a basic standard M1956 web belt has a three-pouch lightweight tropical rucksack built round a steel frame, instead of the usual backpack for the main supplies.

Featured on the web belt are two M16 ammunition pouches (the one on the left with a fragmentation grenade attached), an M16 bayonet, a plastic water bottle in an M1956 cover and a first-aid pouch. By 1968, the M1956 pattern of webbing had been superseded (though not completely replaced yet) by the M1967 Modernized Load-Carrying Equipment, which had many of the M1956 features but used nylon instead of cotton duck and webbing, and aluminium instead of steel and brass.

Date:	1968
Location:	Vietnam

220

SAS Lightweight Combat Pack

Designed by the SAS with the practicalities of operating in hot climates firmly in mind, and designated the SAS Lightweight Combat Pack, it was first used in Borneo in 1966, and proved ideal for use in the deserts of Oman.

Its main advantage lay in the straps and the positioning of the packs. The shoulder straps were made of a broad nylon mesh which provided a breathable carrying system that was particularly light in weight, while the width of the straps distributed the weight more evenly. Suspended from the braces were three dark-olive nylon packs. At chest height, the two outer pouches, mainly used for ammunition, would be worn around the front with the main backpack at the rear, all hooked together by loop and toggle fastenings. Each pouch had a press-stud strap at the bottom for securing to a web belt.

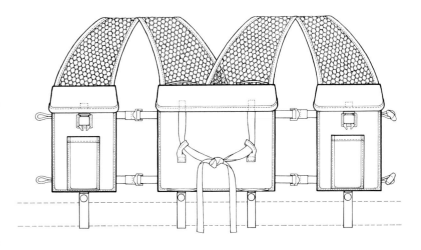

Date:	1973
Location:	Oman

Patriotic Front 'ChiCom' Chest Pouches

The guerrillas of the Zimbabwe African People's Union (ZAPU) were supported by the Soviet Union, China and North Korea in their opposition to the Rhodesian government.

A Chinese influence is apparent in the 'ChiCom' (Chinese Communist) chest pouches, an ammunition-carrying system which was popular in Africa and the Far East. Much of the weaponry used by ZAPU was Soviet or Chinese made, and the three pouches in the centre are for the curved 30-round magazines of the Kalashnikov AK-47 or AKM rifles or the Chinese Type 56 copy. Further ammunition storage would be provided by the smaller pouches on the outside, though these would also contain various accessories such as rifle-cleaning equipment. The chest-pouch system was popular because of its simplicity and comfort under operational circumstances.

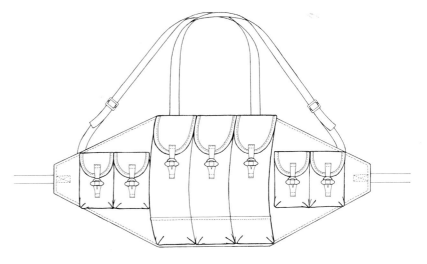

Date:	1979
Location:	Zimbabwe

221

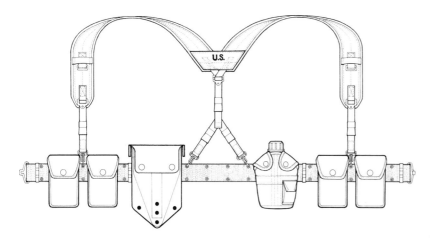

Date:	*1980*
Location:	*El Salvador*

Salvadorean ALICE Version

The Salvadorean Army's battle against the left-wing guerrilla movements in the 1980s was very heavily supported by the US and US Army webbing and equipment was dominant amongst El Salvador's troops.

This system here is recognisably based on the US All-Purpose Lightweight Carrying Equipment (ALICE), though the belt in this case does not have the quick-release plastic buckles of the US issue but retains the M1967 belt clasp. Despite the US aid, the standard firearm of the Army was not the M16 but the 7.62mm West German G3, and the identical pouches at each end of the belt would hold a 20-round G3 magazine. The canteen is the US LC-2 type and the pouch at the front of the cover is for water purification tablets. The final item on the webbing is a folding entrenching tool attached inside a plastic ALICE cover.

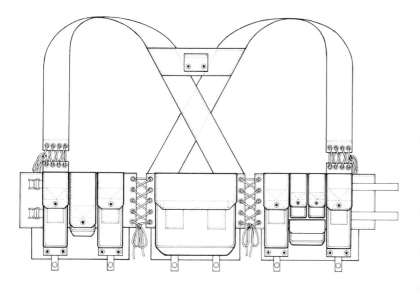

Date:	*1982*
Location:	*Lebanon*

Israeli Paratrooper Load-Carrying Eqpt

This appears to be a cross between standard webbing and a combat vest. It is a comfortable and close-fitting combat carrying system, ideal for the Israeli paratroopers' mixture of land-based and airborne operations.

This Israeli-produced webbing has several unique and distinguishing features, not least the use of laces to attach the broad main straps to the belt and to link the main sections of the belt together. The pouches on the main belt provide the soldier with the versatility to carry a wide range of different supplies and ammunition. The central pack, which fits into the small of the back, is used for basic rations and supplies. The numerous smaller pouches either side of it can contain different ammunition magazines, such as those for the 9mm Uzi and 5.56mm Galil, and many other items of survival, cleaning and operational equipment.

Index

Index